MW01715055

LINDA HILL

The Manifestation Code

A Step-by-Step Blueprint Proven to Transform Your Wants into Reality. Learn to Reprogram Your Beliefs and Unlock the Secrets of Abundant Love, Wealth, and Happiness

MANIFAST™

SCAN THE QR CODE AND MEET YOUR GOAL-SETTING COMPANION

The ManiFAST™ app is here to support you on your journey to achieving your dreams, providing personalized guidance to help you clarify your goals, stay motivated, and track your progress. Whether you're working on personal growth, career ambitions, or daily productivity, ManiFAST™ is designed to keep you focused and inspired every step of the way.

How ManiFAST™ Works

1. **Set Your Goals:** Open the app by scanning the QR Code and signing up! Define your short-term or long-term goals with clear, actionable steps. ManiFAST™ guides you in turning aspirations into achievable milestones.
2. **Receive Daily Motivation:** Get tailored affirmations, productivity tips, and personalized action plans to stay on track. ManiFAST™ keeps you motivated and engaged with tools rooted in evidence-based goal-setting practices.
3. **Track Your Progress:** Monitor your achievements and reflect on your journey. The app offers insights and analytics to help you measure your growth and stay aligned with your vision.

ManiFAST™ is your empowering partner, helping you turn intentions into reality. Take charge of your goals with tools that inspire confidence, clarity, and purpose.

Visit **www.LindaHillBooks.com/ManiFAST** or scan the QR code above for your free access today!

TABLE OF

CONTENTS

5

6

7

8

BOOK DESCRIPTION

Embark on a transformative journey with this comprehensive workbook, designed to unlock your innate ability to shape the life you've always desired. Whether you're starting your manifestation practice or refining your skills, this workbook introduces innovative methods, actionable exercises, and hands-on activities to align your intentions with reality.

Discover how your subconscious mind acts as the architect of your experiences and learn to reprogram it using groundbreaking techniques. With every page, you'll gain tools to break through limiting beliefs, strengthen your inner guidance, and embrace your role as the creator of your reality.

What's Inside?

- **Innovative Methods:** Supercharge your journey with the ManiFAST Method and transformative techniques, designed to turn your intentions into reality with focus and ease.
- **Engaging Exercises:** Hands-on activities such as reflective journaling, crystal alignment routines, and personalized affirmation creation.
- **Quizzes and Key Takeaways:** Reinforce your learning and track your progress with interactive quizzes and concise summaries at the end of every chapter.
- **Tailored Guidance:** Customized practices that adapt to your unique goals, whether they're focused on abundance, relationships, or personal growth.
- **Spiritual Awakening:** Discover the interconnected nature of reality and step into your role as the creator of your life.

ManiFAST™ App + Exclusive Crystal Gift

Your manifestation journey begins with more than just this workbook. Every purchase includes:

- A **carefully selected crystal** to amplify your energy and align with your goals.
- The ManiFAST™ app, your companion tool for:
  - Guided meditations and daily affirmations for consistent alignment.
  - Interactive tools to track progress and maintain focus on your goals.
  - Case studies and testimonials to inspire and provide real-world success stories.

This workbook is more than just a guide—it's your personal map to clarity, confidence, and manifestation mastery. Transform doubt into action, resistance into flow, and potential into purpose. **The life you've dreamed of starts here.**

chapter One

WHY YOU NEED THIS WORKBOOK

INTRODUCTION

Have you ever felt like you're stuck in a cycle—wanting more from life but unsure how to make it happen? Maybe you've tried to change things, but the same struggles keep coming back. If this feels familiar, you're not alone, and this chapter marks the beginning of a journey to shift your reality.

Life can feel overwhelming when you're dealing with challenges like:

- Feeling stuck financially and unsure how to attract abundance.
- Searching for love but doubting whether you'll ever find your soulmate.
- Feeling unfulfilled in your career or uncertain how to achieve success.
- Battling health challenges and wishing for physical or emotional healing.
- Struggling with self-doubt and longing to feel confident and empowered.

These struggles can leave you feeling lost, but here's the good news: manifestation offers a way to transform your reality.

In this chapter, we'll explore what's been standing in your way and how to uncover the powerful potential already inside you. By reflecting on your current reality and comparing it to the life you desire, you'll take the first step toward understanding how manifestation can help.

This Chapter Includes:

- A **Reflection** to help you uncover your biggest pain points.
- **An Exercise** to assess where you are now versus where you want to be, using the app's tools or the journal for offline reflection.
- **A Worksheet** to clarify what manifestation can offer you, available in the app or in the journal for offline use.
- **A Quiz** to identify limiting beliefs, featuring interactive insights on the app.
- **Key Takeaways** with an app-based Q&A feature to reinforce understanding.

Let's get started. By the end of this chapter, you'll have a clearer vision of your goals and a deeper understanding of why manifestation is the tool to get you there.

A CRYSTAL-ENHANCED REFLECTION

IDENTIFYING YOUR PAIN POINTS

Before you embark on your manifestation journey, it's important to take a moment and recognize any obstacles that may be hindering your progress. This exercise, enhanced by the gentle guidance of crystals, will help you uncover and acknowledge the "pain points" – the thoughts, feelings, and patterns that may be limiting you from living your fullest potential.

Choose Your Crystal Companion:

- **Select a crystal that resonates with you.** Some suggestions:
  - **Clear Quartz:** Amplifies intentions and clarity.
  - **Amethyst:** Releases stress and negative emotions.
  - **Black Tourmaline:** Grounds and protects from negative energy.
  - **Selenite:** Clears and purifies the aura.
- **Hold the crystal that resonates with you.** Allow its energy to connect with you as you begin this inner exploration.

Ask Yourself:

Take a few minutes to think about the following questions. Be honest with yourself, and jot down your thoughts. This is your safe space—free from judgment and pressure. The goal is to understand where you are right now.

1. **What feels missing in your life right now?**
   - Is it financial stability, deeper relationships, self-confidence, or something else?
2. **Do you notice problems that continue to repeat over and over?**
   - Are you often stuck in similar situations, like financial struggles or feeling unfulfilled at work?
3. **What emotions come up when you think about these challenges?**
   - Do you feel frustrated, overwhelmed, or unsure about how to move forward?
4. **Have you tried to make changes before? If so, what didn't work?**
   - Were there methods or advice that felt too complicated, impractical, or just didn't resonate with you?
5. **What beliefs do you have about your ability to change your life?**
   - Do you believe change is possible for you, or do doubts and fears hold you back?

Digging Deeper:

Sometimes, the real pain points are hidden beneath the surface. Look at your answers and ask yourself:

- Are these challenges tied to how I view myself or what I think I deserve?
- Could fear of failure or rejection be influencing my actions?

This reflection will give you a clearer understanding of the patterns in your life that need shifting. It's the first step in rewriting your story.

After the Reflection:

- **Journal your insights.** Reflect on the information you've uncovered and consider how it can inform your manifestation journey.
- **Cleanse your crystal.** Gently cleanse your crystal to release any absorbed energies. You can do this by placing it under running water or by smudging with sage to remove any absorbed energies.

This crystal-enhanced reflection will provide you with valuable insights into your current state of being. By acknowledging your pain points and working with the supportive energy of crystals, you can begin to release limiting beliefs and create a more fulfilling and authentic life.

EXERCISE

ASSESSING YOUR CURRENT LIFE VS. DESIRED LIFE

Now that you've identified your pain points, it's time to take a closer look at your current life and compare it to the life you truly desire. This exercise will help you gain clarity on where you are, where you want to be, and what's standing in the way.

STEP 1

Your Current Life

Take a moment to reflect on your current situation. Think about different areas of your life, such as your career, relationships, health, finances, and personal growth. Write down your honest answers to the following questions:

1. What does a typical day in your life look like?
2. How do you feel about your current circumstances?
3. What areas of your life bring you the most stress or dissatisfaction?
4. What do you feel is missing or incomplete?

STEP 2

Your Desired Life

Now, shift your focus to your ideal life. Picture it as vividly as you can—how it looks, feels, and flows. Close your eyes if it helps, and let yourself feel what it's like to live that reality. Then, answer these questions:

1. What does your dream day look like?
2. How do you feel in your ideal life? (e.g., confident, at peace, excited)
3. What does success look like to you in each area of your life?
4. What relationships, achievements, or experiences would bring you joy?

STEP 3

Bridging the Gap

Look at the two lists you've created. Ask yourself:

1. What's the biggest difference between my current life and my desired life?
2. What beliefs, habits, or circumstances are keeping me where I am?
3. What changes would have the most significant impact in moving me closer to my dream life?

VISUAL GUIDE

Use the table below to organize your thoughts:

Area of Life	Current Life Description	Desired Life Description	Gap/Changes Needed
Career			
Relationships			
Health			
Finances			
Personal Growth			

Actionable Insights

Reflect on your answers and choose one area of your life to focus on first. Ask yourself:

- What small, actionable steps can I take right now to move closer to my desired life?

____

____

____

____

____

STEP
4

WORKSHEET
IDENTIFYING YOUR PAIN POINTS

Manifestation is the practice of aligning your thoughts, beliefs, and actions to attract what you desire. This worksheet will help you identify the specific ways manifestation can support your journey and connect your goals to the reality you envision. Use this exercise to clarify how manifestation can bridge the gap between your current life and your desired reality.

Step 1: Identify Your Goals

Let's start by identifying the top three areas of your life—such as career, relationships, health, finances, personal growth, spirituality, hobbies, or social life—that you want to improve or transform. Reflect on the goals or outcomes you deeply desire in these areas, and make them as specific and meaningful as possible.

Area of Life	**Specific Goal or Desire**
Career	Achieve a leadership position within the next six months.
Relationships	Strengthen communication and build deeper connections with loved ones.
Health	Commit to a consistent fitness routine to lose 10 pounds by year-end.

Step 2: Explore the Possibilities

Now that you've clarified your goals, let's dive deeper into how manifestation can support you. Use the journal at the back of this book or the space provided in this exercise to answer the following questions and explore how manifestation can support achieving your desires:

1. What would achieving this goal feel like?
2. What limiting beliefs might be stopping you from reaching this goal?
3. How can you reframe these beliefs into empowering thoughts?
4. How can you exaggerate these beliefs to expand your potential?
5. How could manifestation help you align your mindset with this goal?

Use the template below for each goal:

Goal	What It Would Feel Like	Limiting Beliefs	Reframing	Exaggerating	Manifestation's Role
Example: Financial Stability	Secure and stress-free	"I'll never earn enough money"	"I have enough money."	"I'm going to 100x my money."	Replacing limiting beliefs with affirmations

Step 3: Define Your Why

For each goal, reflect on why it's important to you. Understanding your "why" gives your manifestation process purpose and keeps you motivated.

- **Goal 1:**
  - Why is this goal important to you?
  - How will it change your life?

- **Goal 2:**
  - Why is this goal important to you?
  - How will it change your life?

- **Goal 3:**
  - Why is this goal important to you?
  - How will it change your life?

Step 4: Crafting Affirmations

Manifestation relies on positive affirmations to reprogram limiting beliefs. Based on your goals, write affirmations that resonate deeply with you. For example:

- Goal: Financial Stability
  - Affirmation: "I attract abundance and opportunities effortlessly."

Use this space to write your affirmations or save them in the ManiFAST™ App to enhance them with meditation frequencies.

1. ____
   ____
2. ____
   ____
3. ____
   ____

QUIZ
WHAT'S HOLDING YOU BACK?

This quiz is designed to help you identify the thoughts, beliefs, and habits that may be blocking your manifestation journey.

- Answer honestly—there are no right or wrong answers. The goal is to uncover areas where you can grow and shift your mindset.
- Complete this quiz in the **ManiFAST™ App**, where you'll receive personalized insights and guidance based on your responses.
- Track your progress and revisit the quiz as you grow.

Simply scan the QR code below to access the interactive quiz and begin unlocking your full potential!

Reflection Questions

After reviewing your results, take a moment to reflect:

1. What patterns do you notice in your answers?
2. How have these thoughts or beliefs affected your progress toward your goals?
3. What steps can you take to start shifting your mindset?

Reflection

KEY TAKEAWAYS

Congratulations! You've just taken your first steps toward understanding how manifestation can help you create the life you desire.

Let's reflect on the progress you've made so far. Here's a summary of the key insights and progress you've achieved:

1. **You've Identified Your Pain Points**
    - Recognizing what's been holding you back is the first step to making meaningful changes. By reflecting on your challenges, you've gained clarity about the areas in your life that need attention.
2. **You've Assessed Your Current vs. Desired Life**
    - Comparing where you are now to where you want to be has helped you define the gap between your reality and your goals. You've pinpointed specific areas where manifestation can create positive change.
3. **You've Explored the Role of Manifestation**
    - Manifestation works by aligning your thoughts, beliefs, and actions with your desired outcomes. You've identified how manifestation can help you overcome limiting beliefs and reprogram your mindset for success.
4. **You've Uncovered What's Holding You Back**
    - Through the quiz, you've gained insight into the doubts, fears, and habits that may be hindering your manifestation process. You now have a better understanding of how to shift your mindset and create space for new possibilities.

Access in the App

These takeaways are also available in the **ManiFAST™ App**, where you can engage with interactive Q&A prompts, review personalized suggestions, and track your progress. Scan the QR code below to revisit your progress, stay motivated, and dive deeper into your manifestation journey.

Next Steps

Now that you've laid the foundation, you're ready to dive deeper into the manifestation process. In the next chapter, you'll learn the science and spirituality behind manifestation and begin to explore how your subconscious mind shapes your reality.

Let's continue the journey and move one step closer to the life you deserve!

chapter Two

UNDERSTANDING MANIFESTATION

INTRODUCTION

Let's be honest–manifestation can often feel mysterious or even confusing, especially when you're just starting out. You might wonder, "How does it actually work?" or "Is it really possible to manifest what I want?" This chapter will help demystify the process, giving you a clear understanding of how manifestation blends science and spirituality to shape your reality.

At its core, manifestation is about aligning your thoughts, beliefs, and actions with your desires. But to truly understand it, you need to look at both sides of the equation:

1. **The Science:** How your brain, energy, and subconscious mind work together to create patterns in your life.
2. **The Spirituality:** How universal principles, such as intention and interconnectedness, influence the outcomes you experience.

Here's what you'll gain in this chapter:

- Learn the foundational principles behind manifestation, combining insights from science and spirituality.
- Debunk common myths and misconceptions that might hold you back.
- Explore your personal energy and beliefs through a guided activity.
- Test your understanding with a fun quiz to solidify what you've learned.

By the end of this chapter, you'll have a stronger grasp of how manifestation works and how to apply it confidently to your life. Let's dive in and uncover the truth behind this powerful practice.

Ready to explore this life-changing practice? Let's dive in together!

THE SCIENCE & SPIRITUALITY OF MANIFESTATION

Manifestation is often described as a magical process, but it's deeply rooted in both science and spirituality. Understanding how these two aspects work together can help you approach manifestation with clarity and confidence.

THE SCIENCE OF MANIFESTATION

String Theory and Manifestation

At the heart of modern physics lies string theory, which proposes that the universe's fundamental building blocks are not particles but vibrating strings of energy. These strings vibrate at different frequencies, creating all matter and forces.

In simpler terms, this means everything in the universe—including your thoughts and intentions—is made of energy that vibrates at unique frequencies.When you set an intention, you are essentially tuning your inner vibrations to match those of your desired reality. This alignment allows your thoughts and desires to resonate with the universal strings, potentially influencing outcomes you experience. So, what you think can become real.

Energy and Vibration

Everything in the universe, including your thoughts and emotions, is energy. Science explains this through vibrational frequency—the idea that everything emits a frequency, and like frequencies attract each other. Positive emotions like joy, gratitude, and love resonate at higher frequencies, while fear and doubt vibrate at lower ones.

By consciously focusing on positive energy, you "tune" yourself to opportunities, people, and outcomes that match your desires. This isn't just abstract; it's about shifting your mental and emotional state to align with the life you want to create.

Want to dive deeper? We've curated case studies and related **YouTube videos** that demonstrate these principles in action. Through the **ManiFAST™ App**, you can:

- Watch videos on thought-energy experiments.
- Access detailed explanations of case studies.
- Gain insights into how your thoughts impact your reality.

Simply scan the QR code below to explore these resources and see how science supports your ability to manifest.

THE SPIRITUALITY OF MANIFESTATION

Intention and Interconnectedness

Spiritual teachings across cultures emphasize the power of clear intentions. Think of intention as sending a signal into the universe, aligning events and circumstances to bring that intention to life. This concept is universal, transcending specific beliefs and applying to individuals from all spiritual or non-spiritual backgrounds.

Manifestation has roots in many cultures and religions, illustrating its timeless and inclusive nature:

- **Christianity:** The Bible showcases the power of spoken intention in Genesis 1:3, "Let there be light," where creation begins with a clear command. This reflects the principle of speaking your desires into existence.
- **Taoism:** Taoist teachings emphasize flowing with the Tao (the Way). Aligning one's intentions with the natural rhythms of the universe creates harmony and brings desires to fruition.
- **Hinduism:** The concept of Sankalpa (a heartfelt intention or resolve) highlights the transformative power of focused intent when combined with dedication and mindfulness.
- **Buddhism:** Right intention, a pillar of the Noble Eightfold Path, emphasizes aligning one's thoughts and actions with desired outcomes, fostering mindfulness and deliberate effort.
- **Indigenous Beliefs:** Indigenous traditions worldwide often incorporate rituals, prayers, and ceremonies to set intentions, honoring the interconnectedness of life and the natural world.

These examples highlight that manifestation is not tied to any one religion—it is a universal principle rooted in the belief that thoughts and intentions shape outcomes. Whether through prayer, meditation, or purposeful focus, this strategy aligns your inner energy with external possibilities, making it accessible to anyone, regardless of spiritual beliefs. Manifestation invites you to connect with the world in a way that feels authentic to your unique perspective, blending timeless wisdom with modern practice.

The Role of Faith and Trust

Spirituality often highlights the importance of surrendering control and trusting the process. When you let go of doubt and fear, you create space for your desires to flow naturally into your life. Faith in your ability to shape your reality builds resilience and strengthens your alignment with your goals.

Universal Laws

Manifestation aligns with universal principles that govern the natural flow of life. Two key laws are foundational to the process of manifestation:

- **The Law of Attraction**: Like attracts like—what you focus on expands, and your energy draws similar vibrations into your life.
- **The Law of Cause and Effect:** Your actions create corresponding results, showing that deliberate, aligned effort leads to meaningful outcomes.

When you manifest correctly, everything feels easy and natural, as though life is flowing in harmony with your desires. This sense of "ease" comes from the fact that your subconscious mind is aligned with your intentions, removing resistance and creating a seamless path toward achieving your goals.

Manifestation is not about forcing outcomes or struggling to make things happen—it's about aligning your energy, thoughts, and actions so that the universe works with you. By understanding these universal laws, you can approach your goals with confidence and clarity, knowing that the process will feel intuitive and effortless when done right.

Bringing It All Together

Science and spirituality are not opposites; they complement each other beautifully. String theory shows how energy and vibration connect us to the universe, while spirituality provides the faith and trust needed to guide this process.

Together, they offer a holistic understanding of how your thoughts, beliefs, and energy create your reality. With this knowledge, you can approach the activities in this chapter with confidence, knowing that manifestation is both a practical and profound practice for shaping your life.

COMMON MYTHS AND MISCONCEPTIONS

Manifestation is a powerful practice, but it's often surrounded by myths and misconceptions that can confuse or discourage people. Let's clear up some of the most common misunderstandings so you can approach manifestation with clarity and confidence.

MYTH 1

Manifestation is Magic

The Truth: Manifestation isn't magic; it's about aligning your thoughts, beliefs, and actions with your desires. **Manifestation + Action = Desired Outcome**. Visualization and positive thinking must pair with intentional steps to create focus, alignment, and opportunities that lead to your goals. Manifestation works best when combined with consistent, practical effort.

MYTH 2

You Only Need Positive Thoughts

The Truth: While positivity plays a role, manifestation is about more than just thinking happy thoughts. Your subconscious beliefs and energy need to align with your intentions. Ignoring doubts or fears won't make them disappear; addressing and transforming them is key to manifesting effectively. It's about balancing positive thoughts with inner work, like shifting limiting beliefs and healing emotional blocks.

MYTH 3

Manifestation Only Works for Some People

The Truth: Manifestation is not reserved for a select few. Everyone has the ability to shape their reality because everyone has a mind, energy, and the capacity to align their actions with their desires. If you feel like it doesn't work for you, it's often a matter of addressing hidden blocks or limiting beliefs.

MYTH 4

If It Doesn't Happen Quickly, It's Not Working

The Truth: Manifestation works with **Universal Timing**, meaning results aren't always instant. Your subconscious mind aligns and prepares you for what's best, often bringing growth and unexpected opportunities along the way. Trust the process—what you need will come at the right moment.

MYTH 5

You Must Be Specific About Every Detail

The Truth: While clarity is important, you don't need to obsess over every detail of your goal. Over-specifying can limit the possibilities the universe might bring your way. Instead, focus on the feeling and essence of what you want rather than micromanaging how it should arrive.

MYTH 6

You Can Manifest Without Action

The Truth: While positivity plays a role, manifestation is about more than just thinking happy thoughts. Your subconscious beliefs and energy need to align with your intentions. Ignoring doubts or fears won't make them disappear; addressing and transforming them is key to manifesting effectively.

MYTH 7

Manifestation Is All About Material Wealth

The Truth: Manifestation can help you attract material abundance, but it's also about creating non-material outcomes like emotional well-being, meaningful relationships, and personal growth. The process is about achieving alignment in all areas of life, not just material gain.

MYTH 8

You're Doing It Wrong If Challenges Arise

The Truth: Challenges don't mean you're manifesting incorrectly. Often, obstacles arise to help you grow or redirect you to something even better. They're part of the process, not a sign of failure. Embrace them as opportunities for self-reflection and growth.

By addressing these myths and misconceptions, you can approach manifestation with a clear and open mind. The more you understand how manifestation truly works, the more effective and fulfilling your journey will be.

GUIDED ACTIVITY

EXPLORING YOUR ENERGY AND BELIEFS

Your energy and beliefs are the foundation of manifestation. This activity will help you explore how your thoughts, emotions, and internal energy influence your reality. Consider using a crystal to amplify your intentions and connect with your inner wisdom. With the **ManiFAST™ App**, you can personalize affirmations, pair them with meditation music, and listen to them on repeat to align with your desires.

Scan the QR code below to open the app and personalize your affirmations with calming meditation music.

Step 1: Grounding and Centering with a Crystal

- If you have a crystal, hold it gently in your hand.
- Close your eyes and take a few deep breaths.
- Focus on the rhythm of your breath. Notice the sensation of the air entering and leaving your body.
- Allow yourself to become present in this moment.
- If you are using a crystal, focus on its energy. Does it feel warm, cool, or smooth? Allow its energy to ground you and bring you into the present state of calm awareness.

Step 2: Reflect on Your Energy

- Continue to hold the crystal (if using).
- Tune into how you feel.
- Reflect on the following:
    - Do you often feel energized and optimistic, or drained and doubtful?
    - What emotions dominate your day (e.g., joy, stress, gratitude, frustration)?
    - When thinking about your goals, do you feel excited or anxious?
- Record your reflections in the journal at the back of this book.

Step 3: Identify Limiting Beliefs

We all carry quiet, limiting beliefs that create resistance to achieving your goals. To uncover them:

- Hold the crystal (if you're using one) near your third eye chakra (between your eyebrows).
- Ask yourself:
  - What beliefs do I hold about my ability to succeed?
  - Do I feel worthy of the things I desire?
  - Are there past experiences that make me doubt myself?
- Write your limiting beliefs in the journal at the back of this book. Naming them is the first step toward freeing yourself from them.

Step 4: Set Empowering Affirmations

Create affirmations that align with your goals and help reframe limiting beliefs. Use this template to get started:

"I am [insert positive quality]. I release [insert limiting belief] and embrace [insert empowering belief]. I am open to the abundance flowing into my life."

Step 5: Meditate with Your Affirmations and Crystal

- Hold the crystal (if using) in your hand or place it near your heart or third eye chakra.
- Close your eyes and repeat your affirmations silently or aloud.
- Focus on the intention behind your words and let their energy flow through you.
- Meditate for 5-10 minutes daily to strengthen your connection to your goal.

Step 6: Track Your Energy Shifts

- At the end of each day, note any changes in your emotions, thoughts, or actions.
- Reflect on questions like:
  - Did I feel more aligned with my goals today?
  - What small, positive changes did I notice in my energy or mindset?

QUIZ
MANIFESTATION MYTHS BUSTED

This quiz is designed to test your understanding of manifestation and clear up any lingering misconceptions. Answer each question to see how well you've absorbed the truths about manifestation.

Take this quiz exclusively in the **ManiFAST™ App** for an interactive experience. The app version provides instant feedback, detailed explanations for each answer, and personalized tips to strengthen your understanding.

To get started, scan the QR code below to access the quiz and gain real-time insights and guidance.

Reflection

- How many answers did you get right?
- If you missed any, revisit the **Common Myths and Misconceptions** section to reinforce your understanding.

Reflection

KEY TAKEAWAYS

In this chapter, you've uncovered the truth about manifestation by understanding its foundation in both science and spirituality. Here are the main lessons to carry forward:

1. **Manifestation Combines Science and Spirituality**
    - Science shows how your energy, thoughts, and vibrations interact with the world around you, shaping your reality.
    - Spirituality emphasizes the power of intention, faith, and interconnectedness to align with the universe.
2. **Energy Is Key**
    - Everything in the universe operates on energy and vibration. Aligning your inner energy with your desires creates opportunities for manifestation.
    - Positive emotions and high-frequency vibrations like gratitude and joy are crucial to attracting what you want.
3. **Manifestation Is Not Magic**
    - It requires effort, alignment, and intentional action. Thoughts and feelings alone aren't enough; they must be paired with steps that move you toward your goals.
4. **Common Myths Debunked**
    - Manifestation isn't instant, doesn't work only for some people, and isn't just about material wealth.
    - Challenges and delays are natural and often guide you to something better.
5. **Understanding Your Energy and Beliefs Is Crucial**
    - Your thoughts and beliefs play a significant role in what you attract. Reflecting on and reprogramming limiting beliefs is a key part of successful manifestation.

Access in the App

These takeaways are also available in the **ManiFAST™ App**, where you can engage with interactive Q&A prompts, review personalized suggestions, and track your progress. Scan the QR code to dive deeper into your manifestation journey.

Next Steps

Now that you've built a solid understanding of how manifestation works and cleared up common misconceptions, you're ready to take deeper action. In the next chapter, you'll begin setting the foundation for manifestation by cultivating self-awareness, clarifying your goals, and overcoming limiting beliefs.

Let's move forward with confidence and clarity as we continue this journey toward creating your best life!

chapter Three

SETTING THE FOUNDATION

INTRODUCTION

Manifestation begins with a strong foundation. To create the life you desire, you first need to understand yourself—your thoughts, beliefs, and the intentions driving your actions. Without clarity and self-awareness, it's easy to feel stuck or misaligned. This chapter focuses on helping you build that foundation, so you can align your energy and actions with your goals.

Self-awareness is the cornerstone of manifestation. When you truly understand your emotions, beliefs, and motivations, you can better identify what's holding you back and what truly matters to you. Once you gain this clarity, setting your intentions becomes simpler, and overcoming limiting beliefs becomes possible.

In this chapter, you'll:

- Learn how to cultivate self-awareness and explore what drives your thoughts and behaviors.
- Practice setting clear and powerful intentions that align with your true desires.
- Identify and overcome the limiting beliefs that may be blocking your progress.

By the end of this chapter, you'll have the tools to clarify your goals and build a mindset that supports your manifestation journey. Let's get started with exploring how self-awareness can transform the way you create your reality.

CULTIVATING SELF-AWARENESS

Self-awareness is the foundation of manifestation. It's the ability to recognize your thoughts, emotions, and behaviors and understand how they influence your reality. When you're self-aware, you can identify what drives your actions, uncover hidden patterns, and make intentional choices that are in harmony with your goals.

Why Self-Awareness Matters

Without self-awareness, it's easy to:

- Repeat unhelpful patterns that keep you stuck.
- Set goals based on external pressures rather than your true desires.
- Overlook the beliefs and emotions that silently shape your reality.

By cultivating self-awareness, you gain clarity about what you genuinely want and why. This clarity becomes a guiding force for your manifestation journey, helping you align your energy and actions with your goals.

How to Cultivate Self-Awareness

1. **Pay Attention to Your Thoughts and Feelings**
    - Throughout the day, take note of recurring thoughts or emotions. Are they mostly positive or negative?
    - Ask yourself, "Why am I feeling this way?" or "What's triggering this thought?"
2. **Journal Regularly**
    - Use a journal to explore your inner world. Write about your experiences, feelings, and reflections.
    - Try prompts like:
        - What brought me joy today?
        - What challenges did I face, and how did I respond?
        - What do I want most right now, and why?
3. **Notice Patterns in Your Behavior**
    - Reflect on habits or actions you repeat often. Do they help you move closer to your goals or hold you back?
    - Identify situations where you feel stuck or reactive. What patterns or beliefs might be influencing these responses?
4. **Seek Feedback from Others**
    - Sometimes, the people around you can offer insights into patterns or behaviors you may not notice.
    - Ask trusted friends or family for honest feedback about how you come across or react in certain situations.

5. **Practice Mindfulness**
   - Mindfulness involves being present in the moment without judgment.
   - Spend a few minutes each day observing your breath, thoughts, or sensations to strengthen your awareness. This simple practice strengthens your awareness and helps you stay grounded.

Self-Awareness and Manifestation

The more you understand yourself, the easier it becomes to identify what's holding you back and what truly excites you. Self-awareness allows you to:

- Recognize limiting beliefs that no longer serve you.
- Tune in to your emotions and align them with your intentions.
- Focus on goals that feel authentic and meaningful.

As you deepen your self-awareness, you'll find it easier to make intentional choices that align with your desires, setting the stage for successful manifestation.

EXERCISE

CLARIFYING YOUR INTENTIONS AND GOALS

Manifestation requires clarity. The more specific and intentional you are about what you want, the easier it becomes to align your energy and actions with your desires. This exercise will help you reflect on your goals, understand your motivations, and set clear intentions that truly resonate with you.

Instructions

Complete this exercise directly in the workbook. Use the prompts provided to reflect and write your responses, gaining clarity and focus as you work through each step.

Step 1: Reflect on What You Truly Want

Take a moment to think about the areas of your life where you'd like to see change. Use these prompts to guide your reflection:

- What areas of my life feel unfulfilled or out of alignment?
- What do I want more of in my life (e.g., abundance, peace, love, adventure)?
- What makes me feel excited, joyful, or at peace?

Write down your answers here:

____
____
____
____
____
____

Step 2: Identify Your "Why"

Understanding why you want something gives your intention meaning and purpose. For each desire you've listed, answer these questions:

- Why do I want this?
- How will achieving this goal make me feel?
- How will it improve my life?

Use the template below to organize your thoughts:

Goal	Why Do I Want This?	How Will It Make Me Feel?
Example: Financial Stability	To reduce stress and gain freedom	Secure and confident

Fill out your own goals here:

____
____
____
____
____
____

Step 3: Prioritize Your Intentions

It's easy to feel overwhelmed by wanting to achieve everything at once. To make things more manageable, choose the top three intentions that feel most important and meaningful to you right now. This will give you focus and help you channel your energy into what matters most.

1. ____
2. ____
3. ____

Step 4: Write Your Intentions

Now that you've prioritize your goals, craft clear and specific intentions for each priority goal. Use present-tense language and focus on what you want, not what you don't want. For example:

- Instead of "I don't want to be stressed about money," write "I am financially secure and attract abundance effortlessly."

Write your intentions here:

1. ____
2. ____
3. ____

Step 5: Visualize Your Goals

Take a few moments to close your eyes and visualize each intention as if it has already come true. Imagine what your life looks and feels like in this new reality. Allow the emotions of joy, gratitude, and excitement wash over you as you embrace this vision.

By the end of this exercise, you'll have a clearer understanding of your goals and the intentions that will guide your manifestation journey.

GUIDED PRACTICE
OVERCOMING LIMITING BELIEFS

Limiting beliefs are thoughts and assumptions that create mental and emotional barriers, preventing you from reaching your full potential. These beliefs often operate quietly in the background, shaping your actions and experiences. To manifest effectively, you need to identify and replace these beliefs with empowering ones.

This guided practice will help you uncover limiting beliefs, reframe them, and shift your mindset toward alignment with your goals.

Step 1: Identify Limiting Beliefs

Take a moment to reflect on any negative thoughts or beliefs you have about yourself or your abilities. These limiting beliefs might sound like:

- "I'm not good enough to achieve this."
- "I don't deserve success."
- "Things never work out for me."

Write down at least three limiting beliefs that come to mind:

1. ______________________________

____

2. ______________________________

____

3. ______________________________

____

Step 2: Trace the Source

Now, think about where these beliefs might have come from. Consider past experiences, societal messages, or interactions with others that might have shaped them. For each belief, ask yourself:

- When did I first start believing this?
- Is this belief based on fact, or is it an interpretation of an experience?

Write down the sources of your beliefs here:

1. ____
____
2. ____
____
3. ____
____

Step 3: Reframe the Beliefs

Reframing involves transforming a limiting belief into an empowering one, but it doesn't stop there. To truly expand your mindset, take it a step further and **exaggerate the belief,** pushing beyond your perceived limits. For example:

- **Limiting Belief:** "I'm not good enough to achieve this."
- **Reframed Belief:** "I am capable, worthy, and constantly growing."
- **Exaggerated Belief:** "I am a powerhouse of success, breaking barriers and achieving more than I ever imagined."

Reframe each of your limiting beliefs below:

1. ____
____
2. ____
____
3. ____
____

Step 4: Reinforce the New Beliefs

To solidify your new beliefs, practice these daily. Here are a few ways to reinforce them:

- **Affirmations:** Write down your reframed beliefs as affirmations and repeat them each morning or before bed. For example:
  - "I deserve success and welcome it into my life."
  - "I am strong, capable, and worthy."
- **Visualization:** Imagine living a life where your new beliefs are true. See yourself succeeding, feeling confident, and embracing opportunities.
- **Action:** Take small steps that align with your new beliefs. Prove to yourself that you can succeed by building momentum.

Affirmations:

- Hold your crystal in your hand or place it gently on your heart.
- Write down your reframed beliefs as affirmations, and make it a habit to repeat them each morning or before bed.
- Focus on the crystal's energy amplifying your affirmations as you say them.
- For example:
  - "I deserve success and welcome it into my life."
  - "I am strong, capable, and worthy."

Visualization:

- **Hold your crystal.**
- Imagine living a life where your new beliefs are true. See yourself succeeding, feeling confident, and embracing opportunities.
- **Allow the crystal's energy to enhance your visualizations, making it feel real and within reach.**

Action:

- **Hold your crystal as a physical reminder of your intentions.**
- Take small steps that align with your new beliefs.
- Prove to yourself that you can succeed by building momentum.

Step 5: Let Go of Old Beliefs

Write and **verbalize** a short statement of release to symbolically let go of your old limiting beliefs. Speaking these words out loud with energy and intention helps solidify your commitment to change and aligns your subconscious with your desires.

Example:
"I release the belief that [insert limiting belief] and open myself to new possibilities. I trust in my ability to create a life aligned with my desires."

Take a deep breath, say your statement out loud, and focus on the energy behind your words. Feel the shift as you let go of the old and make room for the new.

Write your release statement here:

____

____

____

____

____

____

By completing this practice, you've taken an essential step toward rewiring your mindset for success. Limiting beliefs no longer have to hold you back—you have the power to replace them with thoughts and beliefs that support your manifestation journey.

QUIZ

HOW CLEAR ARE YOUR INTENTIONS?

This quiz will help you evaluate whether your intentions are clear, focused, and aligned with your desires. The clearer your intentions, the easier it is to manifest what you truly want.

Take this quiz exclusively in the **ManiFAST™ App** for an enhanced experience. The app provides personalized insights and tips to help you refine your intentions further.

To get started, scan the QR code below to access the interactive quiz.

Reflection Questions

- How can you make your intentions clearer and more specific?
- What steps can you take to connect emotionally with your goals?
- Are there actions you can start today to better align with your intentions?

Reflection

KEY TAKEAWAYS

In this chapter, you've built a strong foundation for manifestation by focusing on self-awareness, clarifying your intentions, and overcoming limiting beliefs. Here's what you've accomplished:

1. **Self-Awareness is Key**
   - You explored how your thoughts, emotions, and behaviors shape your reality.
   - By recognizing patterns and understanding your inner world, you've gained clarity about what drives your actions and decisions.
2. **Clarity is Power**
   - You learned the importance of setting clear and meaningful intentions.
   - By defining your goals and understanding your "why," you've taken the first steps toward aligning with your desires.
3. **Limiting Beliefs Can Be Overcome**
   - You identified beliefs that hold you back and traced their sources.
   - Through reframing and daily reinforcement, you've started replacing those beliefs with empowering ones that support your goals.
4. **Intentions Require Alignment**
   - You assessed how clear and aligned your intentions are with your emotions and actions.
   - By creating actionable steps and staying consistent, you're building momentum toward your goals.

Access in the App

These takeaways are also available in the **ManiFAST™ App**, where you can engage with interactive Q&A prompts, review personalized suggestions, and track your progress. Scan the QR code to dive deeper into your manifestation journey.

Next Steps

With a solid foundation in place, you're ready to move deeper into the manifestation process. In the next chapter, you'll explore how the subconscious mind influences your reality and learn techniques to reprogram it for success.

Let's continue this journey with confidence and focus as you step closer to the life you've envisioned!

chapter Four

THE SUBCONSCIOUS AND REALITY CREATION

INTRODUCTION

YYour subconscious mind is the driving force behind much of what you experience in life. Operating quietly in the background, it shapes your perceptions, decisions, and the reality you create. When your subconscious beliefs are aligned with your desires, manifestation feels effortless. But if hidden doubts or fears dominate, they can block your progress without you even recognizing it.

In this chapter, we'll dive deep into understanding the subconscious mind and how it plays a central role in reality creation. You'll explore how your subconscious auto-corrects to protect you and guide you toward growth, even when it doesn't feel that way. This chapter will empower you to identify subconscious blocks and take cautious steps to reprogram your mind for success.

Here's what we'll cover:

- **Understanding Subconscious Auto-Correction:** Learn how your subconscious adjusts your reality, often in surprising ways.
- **Reflection: Rejections as Reflections of the Self:** Explore how rejection often reveals inner beliefs and self-perceptions.
- **Worksheet: Reprogramming Your Subconscious:** Identify limiting subconscious patterns and replace them with empowering beliefs.
- **Quiz: Subconscious Mastery Check:** Test your understanding of the subconscious mind and its influence on your reality.

By the end of this chapter, you'll have the tools to harness the power of your subconscious mind, aligning it with your conscious intentions to create a reality that truly reflects your desires. Let's begin!

UNDERSTANDING SUBCONSCIOUS AUTO-CORRECTION

Your subconscious mind is like the autopilot of your life. It processes your beliefs, habits, and emotions, constantly working behind the scenes to shape your experiences. One of its most fascinating functions is auto-correction—a mechanism where your subconscious adjusts your reality to align with your internal programming.

What is Subconscious Auto-Correction?

Subconscious auto-correction happens when your subconscious mind redirects you, often in ways that may seem frustrating or confusing at first. For example:

- If you hold a deep belief that you're not ready for a certain opportunity, your subconscious may "reject" it by creating obstacles or leading you to make choices that push it away.
- On the other hand, if you believe you deserve success, your subconscious works to steer you toward situations that support that belief, even if it means letting go of what no longer serves you.

This process isn't meant to sabotage you. It's your mind's way of keeping you aligned with the beliefs and values it's been programmed with, whether those beliefs are helpful or not.

How Does It Work?

1. **Filtering Your Perception**
    - Your subconscious filters out information that doesn't match your internal beliefs. For instance, if you believe opportunities are scarce, you may overlook abundant possibilities right in front of you.
2. **Guiding Your Actions**
    - Your subconscious influences the decisions you make, often without you realizing it. If you subconsciously fear failure, you might avoid taking risks, even when they could lead to growth.
3. **Rejection as Protection**
    - When something or someone leaves your life, it may feel like rejection. In reality, your subconscious might be clearing space for something better aligned with your desires. This is your subconscious auto-correction mechanism at work.

Why Subconscious Auto-Correction Matters for Manifestation

Manifestation is about aligning your subconscious mind with your conscious intentions. If your subconscious programming doesn't match your goals, auto-correction will prevent you from fully achieving them. But when your subconscious beliefs are in sync with your desires, this mechanism becomes a powerful tool, gently guiding you toward growth and opportunities effortlessly.

How to Recognize Subconscious Auto-Correction in Action

Ask yourself:

- Have I experienced "rejections" that later led to better opportunities?
- Do I notice repeated patterns in my life that reflect my deepest beliefs?
- Are there situations where I feel "pushed" away from something, only to realize it wasn't truly meant for me?

By observing these patterns, you can start to understand how your subconscious is shaping your reality.

Aligning Your Subconscious with Your Goals

To work with your subconscious auto-correction rather than against it, here are a few steps you can take:

- **Reprogram Your Beliefs:** Replace limiting beliefs with empowering ones (you'll learn how in this chapter).
- **Trust the Process:** Understand that rejections and redirections are often stepping stones to something better.
- **Stay Aware:** Pay close attention to your thoughts and patterns to identify what your subconscious is prioritizing.

Remember, subconscious auto-correction is not your enemy—it's your subconscious guiding you based on what it believes is best. When you intentionally reprogram your mind to align with your goals, this mechanism becomes your greatest ally.

REFLECTION

REJECTIONS AS REFLECTIONS OF THE SELF

Rejection is one of the most painful experiences we encounter, but it's often misunderstood. When someone or something feels out of reach, it's easy to blame external factors—or even ourselves. However, rejection is rarely about the other person or situation. Instead, it often mirrors our internal beliefs and subconscious programming.

By exploring rejection through this lens, we can better understand how rejections may be reflecting your own inner thoughts, fears, or self-perceptions.

Why Rejection Feels So Real

When you experience rejection, it's natural to internalize it as something personal. You might catch yourself thinking:

- "I wasn't good enough."
- "I didn't deserve that opportunity."
- "They don't see my value."

But in reality, rejection is often your subconscious mind protecting you or guiding you toward something better aligned with your true self. It's an auto-correction mechanism that clears the way for growth and better opportunities.

Rejection as a Mirror

Take a moment to reflect on the following questions. Write your answers below to explore how rejection may reflect your inner beliefs:

1. Think of a recent time you felt rejected. What thoughts or emotions came up for you?

____

____

2. Did the rejection trigger any long-standing fears or insecurities? If so, what were they?

____

____

3. How might your subconscious mind have influenced this situation? Were there beliefs or patterns at play?

____

____

____

Reframing Rejection

Rejection often redirects us toward something better. Consider these prompts to reframe your perspective:

- **What lessons did this rejection teach you about yourself?**

- **Looking back, was this situation truly aligned with what you wanted, or was it something you thought you "should" pursue?**

- **How might this rejection create space for something better in your life?**

Release and Trust

To close this reflection, write a release statement to let go of the pain or frustration caused by rejection. For example:

"I release the belief that this rejection defines me. I trust that it is guiding me toward something better and more aligned with my true desires."

Write your own release statement:

Rejection isn't an ending—it's a redirection. By seeing rejection as a reflection of your inner beliefs, you gain the power to adjust your mindset, release limiting thoughts, and trust the process of manifestation.

WORKSHEET

REPROGRAMMING YOUR SUBCONSCIOUS

Your subconscious mind holds the key to shaping your reality, but it's often influenced by old patterns, fears, and limiting beliefs. Reprogramming your subconscious allows you to align your internal programming with your goals and desires, clearing the path for successful manifestation.

This worksheet will guide you through identifying, challenging, and rewriting limiting beliefs to create empowering ones.

STEP 1

Identify Limiting Beliefs

Think about the beliefs you hold about yourself, your abilities, and your potential. Use the prompts below to uncover beliefs that may be holding you back:

- What negative thoughts do I often have about myself or my goals?
- Are there recurring patterns of doubt, fear, or resistance?
- What do I believe about success, relationships, or opportunities?

Write down at least three limiting beliefs:

1. ______________________________

____

2. ______________________________

____

3. ______________________________

____

STEP 2

Trace the Source

Every belief has a story. Reflect on where your limiting beliefs might have come from:

- Was this belief influenced by a specific experience?
- Did someone important in your life reinforce this idea?
- Is this belief a result of fear, failure, or societal expectations?

Write the source or context for each belief:

1. ____
____
2. ____
____
3. ____
____

STEP 3

Challenge the Belief

Ask yourself the following questions for each limiting belief:

- Is this belief objectively true, or is it just a perception?
- What evidence do I have that contradicts this belief?
- How is this belief holding me back?

Challenge each belief and write your insights:

1. ____
____
2. ____
____
3. ____
____

STEP 4

Rewrite the Belief

Transform each limiting belief into an empowering statement, and then take it one step further by exaggerating the belief to push your limits. Use positive, present-tense language to create both realistic and expansive affirmations.

Examples:

- Limiting Belief: "I'm not capable of achieving success."
  - **Empowering Belief:** "I am capable, resourceful, and deserving of success."
  - **Exaggerated Belief:** "I am a visionary leader, creating massive success beyond my wildest dreams."

Rewrite your beliefs here:

1. ____

   ____
2. ____

   ____
3. ____

   ____

STEP 5

Reinforce Your New Beliefs

Repetition and action help reprogram your subconscious. Choose one or more methods to reinforce your empowering beliefs:

- **Daily Affirmations:** Repeat your new beliefs each morning and evening.
- **Visualization:** Close your eyes and imagine living in alignment with these beliefs.
- **Evidence Tracking:** Notice and write down instances where your new belief proves true.

Write a short plan to reinforce your new beliefs:

____

____

____

____

____

____

Reprogramming your subconscious takes time and consistent effort. As you continue, you'll notice how your thoughts, emotions, and actions begin to align with your goals. This alignment will make your manifestation journey smoother and more fulfilling.

QUIZ

SUBCONSCIOUS MASTERY CHECK

This quiz will help you evaluate your understanding of how the subconscious mind influences your reality and identify areas where you can improve your alignment with your goals.

Take this quiz exclusively in the **ManiFAST™ App** for an enhanced and interactive experience. The app provides personalized insights and guidance based on your responses.

To begin, scan the QR code below to access the quiz and start mastering your subconscious.

Reflection Questions

- How many answers did you get right?
- If you missed any, revisit the **Understanding Subconscious Auto-Correction and Worksheet: Reprogramming Your Subconscious** sections for more clarity.
- What steps can you take to deepen your understanding of your subconscious and align it with your goals?

Reflection

KEY TAKEAWAYS

In this chapter, you've gained valuable insights into how the subconscious mind shapes your reality and learned actionable steps to align it with your goals. Here's a summary of the key lessons:

1. **The Subconscious Mind Shapes Reality**
    - Your subconscious beliefs, patterns, and emotions play a significant role in how you experience the world.
    - Subconscious auto-correction redirects your reality to align with deeply held beliefs, often guiding you toward growth.
2. **Rejections Are Reflections**
    - Rejections often mirror inner beliefs, fears, or doubts.
    - By viewing rejection as a redirection, you can embrace it as an opportunity for growth and alignment.
3. **You Can Reprogram Your Subconscious**
    - Limiting beliefs can be identified, challenged, and rewritten into empowering ones.
    - Techniques like affirmations, visualization, and intentional action reinforce new mindset and align your subconscious with your goals.
4. **Understanding Brings Empowerment**
    - Recognizing how your subconscious operates gives you the power to take control of your reality.
    - With clarity and practice, you can align your internal programming with your conscious desires.

Access in the App

These takeaways are also available in the **ManiFAST™ App**, where you can engage with interactive Q&A prompts, review personalized suggestions, and track your progress. Scan the QR code to dive deeper into your manifestation journey.

Next Steps

With a better understanding of how your subconscious mind influences manifestation, you're ready to move forward with confidence. In the next chapter, you'll explore advanced manifestation techniques and practices to further align your intentions, actions, and energy.

Let's continue this journey toward creating the reality you truly desire!

chapter Five

RELATIONSHIPS AS MIRRORS OF THE SELF

INTRODUCTION

Relationships are one of the most profound tools for self-discovery. Whether they bring us joy or present challenges, the people we interact with often act as mirrors, reflecting our inner thoughts, beliefs, and emotions. By examining these reflections, we can gain deeper insights into ourselves and uncover hidden patterns that influence how we connect with others.

In this chapter, we'll explore how relationships reveal the dynamics of our inner world. You'll learn to recognize these reflections, let go of resistance, and trust your subconscious to guide you toward healthier, more fulfilling connections.

Here's what we'll cover:

- **Recognizing Reflections in Relationships:** Understand how the people in your life reflect your inner beliefs.
- **Exercise: Letting Go and Trusting Your Subconscious:** Practice releasing control and embracing trust in your connections.
- **Worksheet: Self-Reflection for Stronger Connections:** Explore how your inner world shapes your relationships.
- **Quiz: What Do Your Relationships Reflect?**: Test your understanding of how relationships act as mirrors.

By the end of this chapter, you'll have the tools to create stronger, more meaningful relationships while deepening your self-awareness. Let's begin!

RECOGNIZING REFLECTIONS IN RELATIONSHIPS

Have you ever noticed how certain people in your life trigger strong emotions, whether positive or negative? This isn't by chance. The relationships you form often act as mirrors, reflecting your inner beliefs, fears, and desires. By understanding this dynamic, you can use relationships as a tool for personal growth and self-discovery.

How Relationships Reflect Your Inner World

1. **Emotions and Triggers**
   - The emotions you feel in relationships—whether joy, love, frustration, or resentment—often reveal what's happening inside you.
   - For example, if someone consistently frustrates you, it might be mirroring a part of yourself you've suppressed or a fear you haven't fully addressed.
2. **Repeating Patterns**
   - Have you ever found yourself caught in the same cycle within relationships—feeling unappreciated or misunderstood?
   - These recurring patterns often point to subconscious beliefs, such as "I'm not worthy of love" or "People always let me down." Recognizing these beliefs is the first step to changing them.
3. **Validation and Expectations**
   - Relationships can reflect how much validation you seek from others. If you find yourself relying heavily on others for approval, it may signal an inner belief that you're not enough on your own.
   - Conversely, if you often feel disappointed by unmet expectations, it might reveal a need to adjust how you communicate your needs.

Questions for Reflection

Take a moment to reflect on these prompts:

1. Think of a relationship in your life that brings you joy. What qualities about this person resonate with your positive beliefs about yourself?

___

___

___

2. Now think of a challenging relationship. What emotions or patterns arise? How might these reflect unresolved beliefs or fears?

___

___

___

3. What repeating themes do you notice in your relationships, and how do they relate to your inner world?

___

___

___

The Power of Awareness in Relationships

Once you recognize that relationships mirror your inner world, you can use this awareness to grow:

- **Positive Reflections:** Celebrate relationships that highlight your strengths and positive beliefs. They show you what's working well in your mindset.
- **Negative Reflections:** Use challenging relationships to uncover and address limiting beliefs or fears. They provide valuable insights into areas where you can grow.

Moving Forward

Recognizing reflections in relationships is about embracing personal responsibility, while letting go of the need to blame others. Every interaction becomes an opportunity to learn more about yourself and align your beliefs with the reality you want to create.

EXERCISE

LETTING GO AND TRUSTING YOUR SUBCONSCIOUS

Letting go of control in relationships can feel challenging, especially when you're attached to specific outcomes. However, trust is a key element in building meaningful connections and aligning your subconscious with positive outcomes. This exercise will guide you in releasing control, embracing trust, and allowing your subconscious to lead you toward healthier relationships.

Step 1: Identify What You're Holding Onto

Reflect on areas in your relationships where you feel the need to control. These could be expectations, fears, or outcomes you're overly attached to. Use the following prompts to explore:

- Is there someone in my life whose actions I'm trying to control or predict?
- Am I afraid of losing a relationship or being rejected?
- Do I feel anxious about how others perceive me?

Write your answers below:

1. ______________________________

____

2. ______________________________

____

3. ______________________________

____

Step 2: Understand the Role of Trust

Ask yourself these questions to explore your relationship with trust:

- What fears come up when I think about letting go of control?
- What would trusting my subconscious and the process feel like?
- How might letting go improve this relationship or bring peace to my life?

Write your insights below:

1. ______________________________
   ____
2. ______________________________
   ____
3. ______________________________
   ____

Step 3: Practice Letting Go

Choose one specific area of a relationship where you'd like to release control. Write a short statement of intention to let go and trust your subconscious to guide the outcome. For example:

"I release my need to control [a specific situation]. I trust my subconscious to guide me toward alignment and growth in this relationship."

Write your intention here:

____

____

____

____

____

Step 4: Visualization Practice

Close your eyes and visualize yourself letting go of control in this relationship. Imagine:

- Feeling calm and confident as you release your fears and expectations.
- Trusting that the universe and your subconscious will bring the best outcome.
- Experiencing the relationship as harmonious and aligned, free from unnecessary pressure.

Spend a few minutes visualizing this peaceful and trusting state.

Step 5: Take One Action Toward Trust

To reinforce this exercise, take one small action that reflects your intention to let go. Examples include:

- Allowing someone else to take the lead in a conversation or decision.
- Reframing a critical thought with one of understanding or acceptance.
- Expressing appreciation for the relationship without expecting anything in return.

Write the action you will take:

____

____

____

____

____

____

WORKSHEET

SELF-REFLECTION FOR STRONGER CONNECTIONS

Building stronger relationships starts with understanding how your inner beliefs and emotions influence the way you connect with others. This worksheet will guide you in examining the patterns, triggers, and dynamics that influence your interactions. By reflecting on these aspects, you can foster more authentic and meaningful connections in your relationships.

Step 1: Examine Your Relationship Patterns

Reflect on recurring themes or dynamics in your relationships. Use the prompts below to identify patterns:

- Do I often experience the same types of challenges in relationships (e.g., feeling ignored, misunderstood, or unappreciated)?
- Are there qualities or behaviors I consistently notice in the people I attract into my life?
- How do my expectations or fears influence my relationships?

Write your reflections here:

1. ____

____

2. ____

____

3. ____

____

Step 2: Identify Your Triggers

Triggers are strong emotional reactions that can reveal hidden beliefs or fears. Think about the following:

- What behaviors or words from others make me feel defensive, hurt, or frustrated?
- Are there situations where I tend to overreact or withdraw?
- How do these triggers connect to past experiences or unresolved emotions?

Write down your triggers and possible sources:

1. ____________________
   ____
2. ____________________
   ____
3. ____________________
   ____

Step 3: Recognize Positive Reflections

Relationships also reflect your strengths and positive beliefs. Take a moment to celebrate the qualities you appreciate in others and how they mirror your inner self.

- What qualities do I admire most in my closest relationships?
- How do these qualities reflect the positive aspects of my own personality or beliefs?
- What do these reflections teach me about my capacity for connection and love?

Write your positive reflections here:

1. ____________________
   ____
2. ____________________
   ____
3. ____________________
   ____

Step 4: Set an Intention for Growth

Based on your reflections, set an intention to improve your relationships and align them with your inner growth. Use this template or create your own:

"I am committed to nurturing relationships that reflect my best self. I choose to release [specific trigger or limiting belief] and embrace [positive quality or behavior]."

Write your personalized intention here:

____
____
____
____
____

Step 5: Take Action Toward Stronger Connections

Consider one action you can take this week to strengthen a relationship or address a pattern you've identified. Examples include:

- Having an open and honest conversation with someone.
- Practicing gratitude by expressing appreciation for a loved one.
- Setting boundaries to create healthier dynamics.

Write your action plan here:

Self-reflection is a powerful tool for transforming relationships. By understanding how your inner world shapes your connections, you can approach your relationships with more awareness, compassion, and intention.

QUIZ

WHAT DO YOUR RELATIONSHIPS REFLECT?

This quiz will help you evaluate how well you understand the concept of relationships as mirrors of your inner self. It will also guide you in identifying areas where you can deepen your self-awareness and improve your connections.

Take this quiz exclusively in the **ManiFAST™ App** for a deeper and more interactive experience. The app provides personalized insights and guidance based on your responses.

To get started, scan the QR code below to access the quiz and explore what your relationships reveal about you.

Reflection Questions

- How many answers did you get right?
- If you missed any, revisit the **Recognizing Reflections in Relationships and Worksheet: Self-Reflection for Stronger Connections** sections.
- Which insights can you use to approach your relationships with more awareness and intention?

Reflection

KEY TAKEAWAYS

In this chapter, you've explored how relationships serve as mirrors of your inner self, offering insights into your beliefs, emotions, and subconscious patterns. Here's a summary of the key lessons:

1. **Relationships Reflect Your Inner World**
   - The people and interactions in your life often mirror your subconscious beliefs, fears, and desires.
   - Positive and challenging relationships alike provide valuable opportunities for self-discovery and growth.
2. **Triggers Reveal Unresolved Beliefs**
   - When you experience strong emotional reactions, or "triggers," they're signals pointing to unresolved fears or limiting beliefs.
   - By examining these triggers, you can uncover and address the patterns that influence your connections.
3. **Positive Reflections Highlight Strengths**
   - Relationships that bring joy and positivity reflect your inner strengths and empowering beliefs.
   - Acknowledging these reflections helps you build confidence and recognize what's working well in your mindset.
4. **Letting Go Strengthens Trust**
   - Releasing control and trusting your subconscious allows relationships to align naturally with your growth.
   - This practice creates space for deeper connections and reduces tension in your interactions.
5. **Self-Awareness is the Foundation of Strong Relationships**
   - By understanding your patterns, triggers, and beliefs, you can approach relationships with greater awareness and compassion.
   - Self-reflection empowers you to improve connections and align your relationships with your true self.

Access in the App

These takeaways are also available in the ManiFAST™ App, where you can engage with interactive Q&A prompts, review personalized suggestions, and track your progress. Scan the QR code to dive deeper into your manifestation journey.

Next Steps

With these insights, you're ready to move forward in your manifestation journey. The next chapter will explore advanced techniques for aligning your energy, beliefs, and actions with your desired outcomes. Let's continue building the life and relationships you've envisioned!

chapter Six

SPIRITUAL AWAKENING AND ENLIGHTENMENT

INTRODUCTION

Spiritual awakening is a profound shift in perception that leads to a deeper understanding of yourself and the world around you. It's the moment when you begin to realize you're not just a participant in life, but as the creator of your reality. This chapter will guide you through the journey of spiritual awakening and how it can transform your manifestation process.

When you awaken spiritually, you realize your thoughts, beliefs, and actions are intricately connected to everything around you. This interconnectedness brings a sense of empowerment and peace, helping you align with your true self and purpose. Through this chapter, you'll explore your role as the creator of your reality, discover the importance of detachment, and strengthen your connection to your inner compass.

Here's what we'll cover:

- **Discovering Your Role as the Creator of Reality:** Understand how your thoughts and beliefs shape your world.
- **Realizing Interconnectedness Through Journaling:** Use reflective journaling to connect with your deeper self and the universe.
- **Guided Practice: Detaching and Finding Your Inner Compass:** Learn to let go of resistance and trust your internal guidance system.
- **Quiz: Are You Aligned with Your True Self?:** Test your awareness of your spiritual alignment.

By the end of this chapter, you'll have the practical tools to embrace your role as the creator of your reality and deepen your connection to your true self. Ready to begin your journey?

DISCOVERING YOUR ROLE AS THE CREATOR OF REALITY

The realization that you are the creator of your reality is at the heart of spiritual awakening. This understanding shifts your perspective from feeling like life happens to you to realizing life happens through you. Your thoughts, beliefs, emotions, and actions form the blueprint for the reality you experience.

How Do You Create Your Reality?

1. **Your Thoughts Shape Your Perception**
   - Your thoughts are powerful—they determine how you interpret and respond to the world. For instance, if you believe the world is full of opportunities, you'll see and act on them. Conversely, if you believe life is full of challenges, you'll focus on obstacles and miss chances for growth.
2. **Beliefs as Subconscious Drivers**
   - Your deeply held beliefs act as a filter, influencing what you notice and attract. If you believe you're not worthy of success, your actions and energy will reflect that belief. This may lead to missed opportunities or self-sabotage.
3. **Emotions Set Your Vibrational Frequency**
   - Emotions are a form of energy, and they play a significant role in shaping your reality. Positive emotions like joy and gratitude emit high vibrations, attracting positive outcomes, while negative emotions like fear and resentment emit lower vibrations, creating resistance that blocks your path to growth.
4. **Actions Manifest Intentions**
   - Manifestation isn't just about thinking or feeling—it's about taking aligned actions. These actions, guided by your beliefs and emotions, are the tangible steps that bring your intentions to life.

The Power of Interconnectedness

Spiritual awakening also reveals that you're not creating reality in isolation. You are connected to the universe and every person, situation, and outcome around you. This interconnectedness means that:

- Your thoughts and energy ripple outward, influencing not only your reality but also the realities of those around you.
- By aligning with universal principles like trust, gratitude, and love, you harmonize with the natural flow of life.

Steps to Embrace Your Role as the Creator

1. **Take Responsibility**
   - Accept that you have the power to shape your reality. Instead of blaming external circumstances, ask yourself: "What thoughts, beliefs, or actions led to this outcome?"
2. **Audit Your Thoughts and Beliefs**
   - Start paying attention to the thoughts you repeat daily. Are they supporting or sabotaging your goals? Challenge and reframe limiting beliefs into empowering ones.
3. **Practice Emotional Awareness**
   - Check in with your emotions regularly. If you notice negative emotions, pause and ask yourself: "What belief or fear is causing this feeling?" Shift your focus to gratitude or a positive affirmation to raise your vibration.
4. **Set Intentions with Clarity**
   - Be specific about what you want to create and why it matters to you. Write your intentions down and visualize them as if they've already come true.
5. **Take Aligned Actions**
   - Align your actions with your intentions. Even small steps in the right direction reinforce your belief in yourself as the creator of your reality.

Affirmation to Embrace Your Role

"I am the creator of my reality. My thoughts, beliefs, and actions shape my experiences. I align with positive energy and trust the universe to support my journey."

Repeat this affirmation daily to reinforce your understanding and empower your creative role.

REALIZING INTERCONNECTEDNESS THROUGH JOURNALING

Journaling is a powerful tool for self-reflection and spiritual growth. It allows you to explore the ways in which your thoughts, actions, and relationships are interconnected with the world around you. This practice helps you deepen your awareness of how you influence your reality and how the universe supports your journey.

In this section, we'll use journaling prompts to uncover patterns of interconnectedness in your life and strengthen your understanding of your role in the greater whole. Through this practice, you'll gain deeper insight into how you are intricately woven into the fabric of life itself.

Why Journaling Helps Recognize Interconnectedness

1. **Clarifies Thoughts and Feelings**
   - Writing down your thoughts helps you see connections between your inner world and external experiences.
2. **Reveals Patterns**
   - Journaling allows you to identify recurring themes in your life, such as the relationships, beliefs, or habits that shape your reality.
3. **Fosters Gratitude and Awareness**
   - By reflecting on moments of synchronicity or alignment, you cultivate a sense of gratitude and connection with the universe.

Journaling Prompts for Interconnectedness

Set aside 10-15 minutes in a quiet space to reflect on the following prompts. Write freely without judgment.

1. Synchronicities and Signs

- Have you noticed moments of synchronicity in your life, such as "coincidences" or signs that guided you? What do these experiences tell you about your connection to the universe?

____

____

____

2. Thoughts and Reality

- Can you think of a time when your thoughts or beliefs directly influenced an outcome in your life? What did this teach you about your power to create?

____

____

____

3. **Relationships as Mirrors**

- Reflect on a recent interaction or relationship. How did this person or experience mirror your own beliefs, fears, or desires?

____

____

____

4. **Moments of Alignment**

- Describe a moment when everything seemed to align perfectly for you. What mindset or actions led to this alignment?

____

____

____

5. **Your Role in the Whole**

- How do you see yourself contributing to the lives of others and the greater world? What unique qualities or intentions do you bring to the collective experience?

____

____

____

Reflection After Journaling

After completing the prompts, take a moment to reflect on what you've uncovered. Ask yourself:

- What patterns or connections stand out to me?
- How do these reflections change the way I see myself and my role in the universe?
- What steps can I take to strengthen my alignment with the interconnected flow of life?

Journaling regularly will deepen your sense of interconnectedness and help you align with the energy of creation. Through reflective prompts and introspection, you can uncover patterns and open yourself to infinite possibilities.

GUIDED PRACTICE

DETACHING AND FINDING YOUR INNER COMPASS

Detachment is a key element of spiritual growth and manifestation. It doesn't mean giving up on your desires—it means releasing the need to control every outcome and trusting your internal guidance system, or "inner compass," to lead you in the right direction. This practice will help you let go of resistance, quiet external noise, and tune into your inner wisdom.

Step 1: Understand Detachment

Detachment allows you to focus on what you want without being consumed by how it will happen. It creates the mental and emotional space needed for the universe to bring you the best outcome, often in ways you couldn't have anticipated.

Reflect on these questions to understand your current relationship with detachment:

- Do I feel anxious or impatient when waiting for results in my life?
- How much do I try to control the people, situations, or outcomes around me?
- Am I open to the idea that the universe may have better plans than I can imagine?

Write your thoughts here:

____

____

____

____

____

____

Step 2: Center Yourself

To find your inner compass, you need to quiet your mind and connect with your intuition. Follow these steps:

1. Sit in a quiet, comfortable space. Close your eyes and take a few deep breaths.
2. Place one hand over your heart and the other on your stomach to connect with your inner self.
3. Focus on your breathing, allowing your body and mind to relax.

Step 3: Tune Into Your Inner Compass

Your inner compass is your intuition—the guiding feeling that remains when distractions fade. In today's noisy world, social media and constant stimulation can drown it out, but with practice, you can sense it clearly. Intuition isn't loud; it's the steady knowing of what feels right and aligned.

Ask yourself:

- What do I feel most drawn to in my life right now?
- Is there something I've been resisting that I need to let go of?
- How does my body feel when I think about this situation or decision?

Write down any insights or feelings that come to you:

____

____

____

____

____

____

Step 4: Practice Letting Go

Imagine holding a balloon in your hand. Visualize placing all your worries, fears, and need for control into the balloon. When you're ready, release the balloon and watch it float away. Feel the weight lifting off you as you let go.

Afterward, affirm to yourself:

"I release the need to control outcomes. I trust my inner compass and the universe to guide me to what is best for me."

Step 5: Take Aligned Action

Detachment doesn't mean inaction. It means moving forward with trust rather than desperation. Choose one small action you can take today to align with your intentions while letting go of the outcome. Examples include:

- Sending an email or making a call without obsessing over the response.
- Starting a project and trusting the process to unfold naturally.
- Expressing gratitude for where you are now.

Write down your chose action:

____

____

____

____

____

____

Step 6: Reflect on the Practice

At the end of the day, take a moment to reflect on how detachment felt for you. Ask yourself:

- Did I feel lighter or more at ease?
- Did any unexpected opportunities or insights come to me?
- How can I continue to trust my inner compass in the future?

By practicing detachment and trusting your inner compass, you align yourself with the flow of life and open the door to unexpected blessings.

QUIZ

WHAT DO YOUR RELATIONSHIPS REFLECT?

This quiz will help you evaluate your connection with your inner compass and determine how aligned you are with your true self. By identifying areas where you might feel disconnected, you can take steps to strengthen your alignment.

Take this quiz exclusively in the **ManiFAST™ App** for an enhanced and interactive experience. The app provides personalized insights and guidance based on your responses.

To begin, scan the QR code below to access the quiz and start aligning with your true self.

Reflection Questions

- What do your answers reveal about your current level of alignment with your true self?
- What steps can you take to strengthen your connection to your intuition and inner compass?
- How can you embrace uncertainty and trust the process more fully?

Reflection

KEY TAKEAWAYS

In this chapter, you've explored the transformative journey of spiritual awakening and learned how to align with your true self. Here's a summary of the key lessons:

1. **You Are the Creator of Your Reality**
    - Your thoughts, beliefs, emotions, and actions shape the reality you experience.
    - Taking responsibility for your inner world empowers you to create a life that reflects your desires.
2. **Interconnectedness Enhances Awareness**
    - Journaling reveals patterns and synchronicities, highlighting your deep connection to the universe.
    - Recognizing interconnectedness strengthens your understanding of how your energy and actions influence the world around you.
3. **Detachment Opens the Door to Alignment**
    - Letting go of control and trusting your inner compass allows life to unfold naturally.
    - Detachment reduces resistance and creates space for unexpected blessings and growth.
4. **Trust and Intuition are Your Guides**
    - Listening to your inner compass helps you navigate life with clarity and confidence.
    - Intuition and trust in the process lead to greater peace, alignment, and manifestation success.

Access in the App

These takeaways are also available in the **ManiFAST™ App**, where you can engage with interactive Q&A prompts, review personalized suggestions, and track your progress. Scan the QR code to dive deeper into your manifestation journey.

Next Steps

With these insights, you are ready to embrace your role as the creator of your reality while remaining open to the flow of life. In the next chapter, we'll explore advanced techniques to deepen your manifestation practice and accelerate your alignment with your goals.

Let's continue this journey toward a more awakened and empowered self!

chapter

Seven

ADVANCED MANIFESTATION TECHNIQUES

INTRODUCTION

Manifestation is a journey of growth and alignment. As you progress, you may find that foundational techniques provide a solid base, but advanced practices can unlock deeper levels of clarity and success. This chapter is designed to help you explore powerful, next-level tools and methods that amplify your manifestation process, aligning your thoughts, energy, and actions with precision.

In this chapter, we'll dive into advanced manifestation techniques tailored to enhance your focus, creativity, and alignment. These methods go beyond basic visualization and affirmations, introducing tools that engage your subconscious mind, refine your energy, and supercharge your intentions. Whether you're looking to deepen your meditation practice, create a compelling vision board, or incorporate innovative techniques, this chapter equips you with strategies to transform your goals into reality.

In this chapter, you'll:

- **The ManiFAST Manifestation Method:** A groundbreaking approach to harmonizing your energy and intentions.
- **Vision Board Creation:** Designing a visual roadmap to manifest your desires.
- **Enhanced Meditation Techniques:** Leveraging mindfulness for manifestation success.
- **Reflection and Practice:** Activities to identify and align with the methods that resonate most.
- **Key Takeaways and Quiz:** Reinforce your learning and discover your most effective tools.

By the end of this chapter, you'll have a toolkit of advanced techniques to expand your manifestation potential and align more deeply with your goals. Let's take your practice to the next level!

THE MANIFAST MANIFESTATION METHOD EXPLAINED

The ManiFAST Method is your step-by-step guide to mastering manifestation. By combining intention-setting, energy alignment, and inspired action, this method ensures that every part of your manifestation journey is purposeful and effective. Central to this method is the Manifestation Equation, which is a simple but powerful formula that breaks manifestation into actionable steps. To enhance this process, we'll also integrate the energy-amplifying power of crystals. Together, they create a system designed to help you achieve your goals with focus and ease.

Manifestation Equation

M = (I + E + C)^A × F

Where:

- **M** = Manifestation (the desired outcome)
- **I** = Intention (clarity of what you want)
- **E** = Emotional Energy (positive feelings and belief that it will happen)
- **C** = Consistent Action (aligned steps toward the goal)
- **A** = Alignment (the harmony between your thoughts, emotions, and actions)
- **F** = Focus (the sustained attention you give to your goal)

How the ManiFAST Method Works

The ManiFAST Method works in three interconnected phases: Intention Setting, Energy Alignment, and Inspired Action. Each phase uses the Manifestation Equation and the unique energetic properties of crystals to help you turn your desires into reality.

Phase 1: Intention Setting (I)

Manifestation starts with clarity. When you're specific about what you want, it becomes much easier to attract it. Crystals amplify this clarity, helping you stay focused on your goals.

Steps for Intention Setting:

- **Be Specific:** Define your goal with precision.
  - Example: "I am earning $5,000 within the next three months."
- **Align with Your Values:** Ensure your goal resonates with your true self.
  - Example: "I am building financial freedom to support my passions."
- **Use Present-Tense Affirmations:** Affirm your goals as if they're already achieved.
  - Example: "I am attracting $5,000 effortlessly this month."
- **Program Your Crystal:** Choose a crystal, such as Citrine for abundance or Rose Quartz for love. Hold it, focus on your goal, and affirm:
  - "I program this crystal to amplify my intention for [your specific goal]."

Phase 2: Energy Alignment (E + A)

This phase focuses on ensuring your emotions and energy resonate with your desires. Crystals help you maintain this alignment by acting as energetic amplifiers.

Steps for Energy Alignment:

- **Visualize with Feeling**: Hold your crystal while imagining your goal as already achieved. Feel the emotions of success.
- **Practice Gratitude:** Be thankful daily, even for the things you're manifesting. Gratitude aligns your energy with abundance.
- **Clear Blockages:** Use crystals like Black Tourmaline to release fears or limiting beliefs through journaling or mindfulness.
- **Harmonic Resonance:** Meditate with sound frequencies (e.g., 528 Hz) while keeping your crystal nearby to amplify alignment.

Phase 3: Inspired Action (C + F)

Manifestation requires more than just thought—it requires action. Crystals serve as reminders to take consistent, aligned steps toward your goals.

Steps for Inspired Action:

- **Listen to Your Intuition:** Trust the nudges and insights that come to you. Use your crystal as a grounding tool.
- **Take Small, Aligned Steps:** Even small, consistent actions can lead to big results.
- **Celebrate Wins:** Acknowledge your progress and use Clear Quartz to amplify positive energy during these moments.

Crystals: Your Manifestation Allies

Crystals are an essential part of the **ManiFAST Method**, acting as tools to anchor your intentions and magnify your energy. Each crystal has unique properties to support specific goals:

- **Clear Quartz:** Amplifies focus and intentions.
- **Citrine:** Attracts abundance and success.
- **Amethyst:** Promotes calmness and intuition.
- **Rose Quartz:** Supports love and emotional healing.
- **Black Tourmaline:** Grounds and protects energy.

How to Use Crystals in the ManiFAST Method:

- **Cleanse Your Crystal:** Purify its energy with water, sage, or sunlight.
- **Program Your Crystal:** Infuse it with your intention during Phase 1.
- **Incorporate It Daily:** Carry it, meditate with it, or place it where you can see it regularly.

Why the ManiFAST Method Works

The **ManiFAST Method** is designed to help you manifest effectively by combining clarity, alignment, and action. The Manifestation Equation provides structure to your journey, while crystals amplify your focus and energy, ensuring every step is purposeful and aligned with your desires.

For the best results, use this workbook alongside the **ManiFAST™ App**. The workbook helps you reflect and build your foundation, while the app takes your practice to the next level with tools like guided meditations, harmonic frequencies, and progress tracking.

Try it now on the **ManiFAST™ App** to unlock the full potential of your manifestation journey. Ready to begin? Scan the QR code below to get started!

ACTIVITY

APPLYING THE MANIFESTATION EQUATION

This activity will guide you step-by-step to use the **Manifestation Equation (M = (I + E + C)^A × F)** and align all aspects of your manifestation journey. Follow the prompts below to work through each component of the equation,

STEP 1

Define Your Goal (M = Manifestation)

Write down one specific goal or desire you wish to manifest. Be as clear and concise as possible.

- Example: "I want to save $10,000 for a dream vacation within 6 months."

Your Goal:

____

____

STEP 2

Set Your Intention (I = Intention)

Clarify your goal by answering the following:

- What exactly do you want?
- Why is it important to you?
- How will achieving it make you feel?

Your Answers:

____

____

STEP 3

Align Your Emotional Energy (E = Emotional Energy)

- Visualize achieving your goal. Write down how it feels to have it in your life.
- Practice gratitude: List three things you're grateful for that align with your goal.

Visualization Feelings:

____

Gratitude List:

1. ______________________________

____

2. ______________________________

____

3. ______________________________

____

Plan Consistent Actions (C = Consistent Action)

STEP 4

- Example: Open a savings account, automate monthly savings, cut unnecessary expenses.

Your Action Steps:

1. ______________________________
2. ______________________________
3. ______________________________

STEP 5

Ensure Alignment (A = Alignment)

Check if your thoughts, emotions, and actions are consistent with your goal. Use these questions to reflect:

- Are my beliefs supporting or hindering my goal?
- Do I feel emotionally connected to my goal daily?
- Are my actions leading me closer to my goal?

Reflection:

____

____

Maintain Focus (F = Focus)

STEP 6

- Identify one way to remind yourself daily of your goal.
- Example: Create a vision board, use affirmations, or carry a crystal associated with your goal.

Daily Focus Reminder:

____

____

Bonus: Use Crystals to Amplify the Equation

Choose a crystal to anchor your manifestation practice. Program it with your intention and keep it nearby during your activities.

- Example: Use Citrine for abundance or Rose Quartz for relationships.
-

Your Chosen Crystal:

____

____

____

By completing this activity, you'll integrate every component of the Manifestation Equation into your practice, aligning your thoughts, emotions, and actions for success.

ACTIVITY

CREATING YOUR VISION BOARD

A **Vision Board** is one of the most powerful tools for manifesting your desires because it keeps your goals front and center, constantly reminding you of what you're working toward. Think of it as a physical or digital representation of your dreams, using images, words, and symbols to visualize and align your energy with your desires

By creating a Vision Board, you are physically manifesting your goals in a way that engages both your mind and emotions. When you look at it, you are reminded not only of your dreams but also of the powerful energy you are sending out into the universe.

Why Create a Vision Board?

- **Clarify Your Goals:** It helps you define and visualize what you truly want in life.
- **Align Your Energy:** A Vision Board keeps your energy aligned with your goals, reinforcing them daily.
- **Increase Focus:** It serves as a constant reminder to stay focused on what you're manifesting, keeping distractions at bay.
- **Feel Empowered:** Each time you interact with your Vision Board, you feel more connected to your desires, boosting your confidence and belief in your ability to manifest them.

Steps to Create Your Vision Board

STEP 1

Gather Materials

To create a physical Vision Board, you'll need:

- A poster board, corkboard, or canvas (or a digital board if you prefer).
- Magazines, printed photos, or online images that represent your goals (e.g., pictures of a dream home, career goals, travel destinations, health goals, etc.).
- Scissors, glue, or tape.

STEP 2

Get Clear on Your Goals

Before you start cutting out images or collecting photos, take a moment to reflect on what you truly want to manifest. Are your goals related to career, relationships, health, or finances? The clearer you are, the easier it will be to gather images that align with your desires.

Ask yourself:

- What do I truly want to achieve?
- What do I want my life to look like in 3 months, 1 year, 5 years?
- What feelings or emotions do I want to manifest in my life?

STEP 3

Collect and Select Your Images

Now, start gathering images that represent your goals. They don't need to be perfect—just images that evoke positive emotions and excitement. For example, if your goal is to travel the world, find pictures of places you want to visit. If your goal is to improve your health, collect photos of healthy foods, workouts, or calming environments.

STEP 4

Arrange and Glue

Now comes the fun part—arranging your vision board! Once you've gathered your images, start arranging them on your board. There's no wrong way to do this—it's about what feels right to you. Place the most important goals in the center or create a flow that makes sense. Once you're satisfied with the arrangement, glue or pin everything down. Watch your vision come to life as you go!

STEP 5

Place Your Vision Board in a Visible Spot

The magic of a vision board lies in seeing it daily. Find the perfect spot —put your Vision Board somewhere you will see it often—on your bedroom wall, office desk, or even as a digital wallpaper. The key is to engage with it daily. The more you see your goals, the more your subconscious mind will align with them.

Making Your Vision Board Even More Powerful

- **Infuse it with Emotion:** As you look at your Vision Board, feel the emotions of already having achieved your goals. This emotion is what amplifies your manifestation power.
- **Use Affirmations:** Write affirmations on your board that reinforce your goals. For example, "I am attracting abundance" or "I am living a healthy, balanced life."
- **Regularly Update Your Board:** As your goals evolve or you accomplish things, update your Vision Board. Keep it fresh and aligned with your current desires.

Creating a vision board is a powerful manifestation tool that visually represents the life you are creating. By consistently engaging with it, you reinforce your belief that your goals are already on their way to you.

Tips for Building Your Vision Board:

- **Keep It Simple:** A vision board doesn't need to be elaborate. It can be as simple as setting your phone's background or lock screen to a picture that symbolizes what you want.
- **Be Specific:** Use images that clearly represent your desires—whether it's a dream house, career milestone, or a feeling of joy and abundance.

How It Works:

Your vision board acts as a daily reminder of the life you're creating. Whether it's a physical board, a digital version, or your phone's wallpaper, you align your thoughts and emotions with your goals. This consistent exposure reinforces your belief and focus, helping your desires manifest faster.

Let your vision board inspire you every day and remind you that you are actively building the future you deserve!

ENHANCING MEDITATION FOR MANIFESTATION

Meditation is a powerful tool in any manifestation practice. It helps you quiet your mind, align your energy, and deeply connect with your desires. However, in order to take your manifestation practice to the next level, you need to enhance your meditation routine to make it more focused and effective. In this section, we'll explore how to optimize meditation to accelerate your manifestation journey.

Why Meditation is Essential for Manifestation

Meditation allows you to:

- **Clear Mental Clutter:** When your mind is filled with distractions or negative thoughts, it's difficult to manifest. Meditation helps clear this clutter, creating space for your desires to take root.
- **Align Your Energy:** Your thoughts, emotions, and actions need to be in harmony for manifestation to occur. Meditation brings you into a state of alignment where you can attract what you want.
- **Increase Vibration:** Manifestation works on the principle of energy vibration. When you meditate with positive intention, you raise your vibrational frequency, which draws your desires closer to you.

How to Enhance Your Meditation Practice

To truly enhance your meditation and make it a powerful tool for manifestation, you can use the following strategies:

1. Set a Clear Intention Before Meditating

Before you start your meditation session, take a moment to clearly set your intention. This could be anything from manifesting a new opportunity, improving your health, or attracting more abundance into your life. When you set a clear intention, it helps your mind and body stay focused on that goal during your meditation.

Example:

- "I am open and ready to receive new opportunities for success."
- "I am attracting positive energy and abundance into my life."

2. Focus on Your Breath to Calm Your Mind

To reach a deep meditative state, it's essential to calm your mind. Begin by focusing on your breath:

1. Inhale slowly through your nose for a count of four.
2. Hold your breath for a count of two.
3. Exhale slowly through your mouth for a count of six.

This rhythmic breathing slows mental chatter and brings your body into a relaxed state, helping you align with your desires more effectively.

Advanced Techniques

As you grow comfortable with basic breathing techniques, you can explore more advanced practices like **diaphragmatic breathing** (stomach breathing). This approach deepens relaxation and increases focus, making it even easier to align with your intentions.

For step-by-step guidance, access the app now. Simply scan the QR code to learn how to practice these techniques and enhance your meditation sessions.

3. Visualize Your Desires in Detail

Once your mind is calm, begin to visualize your goal in vivid detail. Imagine yourself already living the reality you desire. Engage all your senses—what do you see, hear, feel, and smell in this new reality? The more detail you can include, the stronger the emotional connection, which enhances the manifestation process.

Example:
If your goal is to manifest a new job, imagine yourself walking into the office, feeling confident, and hearing your new colleagues greet you. See the tasks you'll be working on, feel the excitement of success, and hear the positive feedback from your boss.

4. Use Affirmations to Strengthen Your Focus

Affirmations are an excellent tool to reinforce your intentions and align your thoughts with your desires. As you meditate, repeat positive affirmations related to your goals. These affirmations should be in the present tense, as though your manifestation is already happening.

Example Affirmations:

- "I am attracting limitless abundance into my life."
- "I am living a life full of love, peace, and fulfillment."
- "I am healthy, vibrant, and full of energy."

5. Practice Gratitude

Ending your meditation with gratitude amplifies its impact. Feel thankful for the manifestations that are already on their way to you. Gratitude raises your vibrational frequency, aligning you even more closely with your desires.

Example:

- "I am so grateful for the abundance in my life."
- "I am thankful for the love and support surrounding me."

6. Meditate Regularly to Strengthen Your Manifestation Muscle

The more consistently you meditate, the stronger your manifestation practice becomes. Try to meditate at least once a day, even if it's just for a few minutes. The key is to stay consistent and make it a daily habit to keep your energy aligned with your goals.

Enhancing your meditation practice can significantly improve the manifestation process. By using intention, breathwork, visualization, affirmations, and gratitude, you are amplifying your energy and aligning with your desires more effectively. With consistent practice, you'll begin to notice shifts in your reality, bringing you closer to your goals.

Now that you've explored the ManiFAST Manifestation Method and enhanced your meditation practice, it's time to reflect on which manifestation technique works best for you. Understanding your unique approach will help you align with the techniques that resonate most, making your manifestation practice even more effective.

QUIZ

WHICH TECHNIQUE FITS YOU BEST?

This quiz will help you discover which manifestation technique aligns most with your current mindset and goals. By identifying the approach that resonates with you, you can personalize your practice for maximum effectiveness and alignment with your true desires.

Take this quiz exclusively in the **ManiFAST**™ App to gain detailed insights and personalized guidance based on your responses. Simply scan the QR code below to access the interactive quiz and start tailoring your manifestation journey.

Reflection Questions

- What do your answers reveal about your current level of alignment with your true self?
- What steps can you take to strengthen your connection to your intuition and inner compass?
- How can you embrace uncertainty and trust the process more fully?

Reflection

KEY TAKEAWAYS

1. **The ManiFAST Manifestation Method** combines intention-setting, energy alignment, and inspired action, offering a comprehensive approach to manifestation that helps you achieve your goals with clarity and purpose.
2. **Creating a Vision Board** is a powerful tool for visualizing your desires. By engaging with your board regularly, you reinforce your goals and maintain focus on what you're manifesting.
3. **Enhancing your meditation practice** helps align your energy with your desires. By incorporating intention, breathwork, visualization, and gratitude, you can amplify your manifestation abilities.
4. **Choosing the right technique** for your personality is essential. Whether you thrive on structure, intuition, or surrender, aligning your manifestation practice with your natural approach will lead to greater success.
5. **Detaching from the outcome** and trusting your inner compass allows the universe to work its magic. Surrendering control and embracing uncertainty are key to manifesting effortlessly.

Access in the App

These takeaways are also available in the **ManiFAST™ App**, where you can engage with interactive Q&A prompts, review personalized suggestions, and track your progress. Scan the QR code to dive deeper into your manifestation journey.

Next Steps

With the insights and techniques, you've laid the foundation for powerful manifestation. Now that you understand how to align your energy, set intentions, and take inspired action, it's time to take things further.

In **Chapter 8**, we'll dive into **hands-on activities** designed to deepen your manifestation practice. These activities will allow you to engage with manifestation on a more physical level, strengthening your connection to your goals and accelerating your results.

Let's continue this transformative journey toward manifesting your desires with even greater clarity and purpose!

chapter

Eight

ACTIVITIES TO ENHANCE MANIFESTATION (HANDS-ON SECTION)

INTRODUCTION

Manifestation is not just about setting intentions—it's about taking consistent, intentional action that aligns your energy, thoughts, and goals. In this chapter, you will discover hands-on activities that are specifically designed to enhance your manifestation practice. These activities provide practical, experiential tools that bridge the gap between your desires and their realization.

Each exercise focuses on a unique aspect of the manifestation process, whether it's cultivating clarity, raising your energy, or refining your focus. By incorporating these activities into your daily routine, you will strengthen your ability to manifest with precision and confidence. Additionally, you'll explore how **combinations of techniques** can amplify results, creating powerful synergies that accelerate your progress.

Here's what you can expect:

- **Mind Resetting:** Simple techniques to reduce mental chatter and enhance your ability to focus, allowing you to connect with your inner wisdom and manifest your desires.
- **Sunrise Journaling:** A reflective exercise to connect with your intentions through sun gazing.
- **Breath Aligning Practice:** Breathwork techniques for harmonizing your mind and body.
- **Biofeedback:** Tools for tracking your manifestation progress with advanced neurofeedback methods.
- **Red Light Journaling:** A daily practice to integrate the benefits of Red Light Therapy.
- **Earth Journaling:** Grounding exercises to reconnect with nature and realign your energy.
- **Energy Cultivation Practices:** Movements inspired by Tai Chi to balance your physical and mental state.
- **Meditative Journaling:** Guided prompts to deepen your meditation practice and self-awareness.
- **Self Manifestation:** A goal-setting framework for creating clear, actionable steps.
- **Collective Manifestation:** A collaborative exercise to magnify intentions through collective energy.
- **Visualization Method:** Techniques to visualize and map out your manifestations vividly.
- **Affirmations Embedding Method:** Activities to create affirmations that align with your goals with sound-based techniques to align your energy with your desires.

By engaging with these activities, you're not just learning—you're actively manifesting. The more you immerse yourself, the more you'll notice synchronicities, growth, and alignment unfolding in your life.

Let's get hands-on and bring your manifestations to life!

MIND RESETTING

Mind Resetting techniques provide a gentle pathway to clear the mind, quiet mental chatter, and cultivate a state of inner peace. By calming the mind, you create the ideal space for focused intention and effortless manifestation.

How It Works

Mind Resetting often involves practices that encourage a gentle detachment from thoughts and overthinking. These techniques help to:

- Reduce mental chatter: Calm and ease the constant stream of thoughts that often cloud your mind.
- Increase present moment awareness: Cultivate a deeper connection to the present experience.
- Access a state of inner stillness: Experience a sense of peace and tranquility beyond thought.

Steps to Practice Sunrise Journaling:

1. **Find Your Space:** Choose a quiet and comfortable space where you can relax without distractions. Close your eyes and gently detach from your surroundings.
2. **Focus on Darkness:** With your eyes closed, allow your attention to rest on the darkness behind your eyelids. Allow your mind to rest in this quiet space. Notice any thoughts or feelings that arise without engaging with them.
3. **Reflect (Optional):** After your practice, gently observe any thoughts or emotions that linger. Journal about your experience if desired, but without forcing any particular outcome.
4. **Express Gratitude:** Conclude your practice by expressing gratitude for the opportunity to connect with a deeper level of stillness within yourself.

Tips for Success:

- Start with short sessions: Begin with 5-10 minutes of practice and gradually increase the duration as you become more comfortable.
- Be patient and compassionate with yourself: It's natural for thoughts to arise during meditation. When they do, gently guide your attention back to the present moment without judgment.
- Incorporate into your daily routine: Practice Mind Resetting techniques regularly, such as before meditation, affirmations, or visualization exercises.

Why it Works

By quieting the mind, you improve sleep, boost creativity, and gain access to deeper insights. This state of inner calm helps you strengthen self-awareness, foster intentionality, and pave the way for manifesting your desires with clarity and confidence.

SUNRISE JOURNALING

Harnessing the energy of the sun can be a transformative way to align your mind, body, and spirit. **Sunrise Journaling** combines the benefits of sunlight with intentional reflection, helping you clarify your goals and strengthen your connection to your desires.

How It Works

Sun gazing involves observing the sun during the first hour after sunrise or the last hour before sunset—times when sunlight is softer and safer for your eyes. Pairing this with journaling allows you to ground yourself in the present moment, clear mental fog, and receive inspiration for your manifestation journey.

Steps to Practice Sunrise Journaling:

1. **Find Your Space:** Choose a quiet outdoor location with an unobstructed view of the sun. Bring your journal and a pen.
2. **Set Your Intention:** Before starting, take a deep breath and set a clear intention for your practice. For example: "I open myself to clarity, inspiration, and alignment."
3. **Sun Gazing:** Softly gaze at the sun for 1-3 minutes. Focus on its warmth, light, and energy as it connects with you.
4. **Reflect and Write:** After sun gazing, close your eyes and tune into any feelings, ideas, or insights that arise. Begin journaling with prompts like:
   - What thoughts or images came to me during this practice?
   - What am I inspired to focus on today?
   - How can I align my energy with my intentions?
5. **End with Gratitude:** Conclude your practice by expressing gratitude for the sunlight, your insights, and the energy you are cultivating.

Tips for Success:

- Practice during sunrise or sunset to ensure safety and maximize the calming effects.
- Keep your journal entries free-flowing; this is a space for inspiration, not perfection.
- Combine this exercise with affirmations or a meditation session for deeper alignment.

Why it Works

Sunlight is a natural source of energy that uplifts your mood, enhances focus, and strengthens your connection to the present moment. By pairing this practice with journaling, you create a powerful synergy that allows clarity and inspiration to flow effortlessly.

Take time to immerse yourself in the energy of the sun and watch how your intentions come alive on the page. Let the light guide your manifestation journey!

BREATH ALIGNING PRACTICE

Breathing is one of the most powerful tools for aligning your mind, body, and energy. The **Breath Aligning Practice** focuses on intentional breathwork to reduce stress, clear mental clutter, and bring your mind into harmony with your intentions. This activity helps you regulate your energy flow and create a foundation for effective manifestation.

How It Works: The 4-7-8 breathing technique is a simple yet impactful practice that balances your nervous system, calms your thoughts, and promotes a state of relaxation—all essential for aligning with your goals.

Steps to Practice Breath Aligning Practice:

1. **Find a Quiet Space:** Sit comfortably in a peaceful environment, ensuring you won't be disturbed.
2. **Set Your Intention:** Focus on an intention that brings you calm and clarity. For example: "I allow my energy to flow freely and harmoniously."
3. **Breathe with the 4-7-8 Method:**
   - Inhale deeply through your nose for 4 seconds.
   - Hold your breath for 7 seconds.
   - Exhale slowly and fully through your mouth for 8 seconds, imagining negative energy and stress flowing out with each breath.
   - Repeat this cycle 4-6 times.
4. **Log Your Experience:** After completing the breathwork, reflect on your experience with prompts like:
   - How did my body feel before and after the practice?
   - What thoughts or emotions surfaced during the exercise?
   - How can I carry this sense of calm into the rest of my day?
5. **Track Your Progress:** Create a log to note the date, time, and any insights you gain from each session. Over time, observe how regular breathwork influences your ability to manifest with clarity and focus.

Tips for Success:

- Practice this method at the start of your day to set a calm, focused tone or before bed to release stress and tension.
- Pair the 4-7-8 technique with affirmations or visualization for amplified results.
- Consistency is key—a regular breathwork practice deepens its impact on your energy and mindset.

Why It Works: Breathwork regulates the parasympathetic nervous system, reducing stress and calming the mind. This creates the ideal internal environment for manifestation by allowing your energy to align with your goals effortlessly.

Take a few moments to breathe deeply, align your energy, and pave the way for your intentions to manifest with ease.

BIOFEEDBACK

Manifestation thrives when you track your growth and progress. The **Biofeedback** introduces a powerful way to observe and measure your energetic alignment and manifestation journey using neurofeedback techniques.

How It Works

Neurofeedback methods train your mind to recognize and shift its patterns, helping you achieve states of focus, calm, and clarity. By tracking your mental and emotional states, you can monitor how aligned you are with your manifestation goals.

Steps to Practice Biofeedback:

1. **Choose Your Tracking Tool:** You can use a neurofeedback app, wearable device, or a simple journal to monitor your focus, mood, or emotional states.
2. **Set Your Baseline:** Spend 5-10 minutes observing your current state without judgment. Note how you're feeling mentally, physically, and emotionally.
3. **Focus on Your Intentions:** Engage in a brief manifestation practice (e.g., visualization, affirmations, or meditation) while monitoring your mental state.
4. **Record Your Observations:** Use prompts like:
    - What shifts did I notice in my focus or emotions during this session?
    - How clear and energized do I feel about my intentions right now?
    - What patterns am I beginning to recognize?
5. **Track Progress Over Time:** Create a chart to log each session's observations. Include areas like focus level, emotional state, and physical energy. Watch for trends and improvements as you practice.

Tips for Success:

- Try this practice when feeling overwhelmed or unfocused to regain clarity.
- Pair neurofeedback tracking with visualization exercises for enhanced results.
- Consistency matters—regular tracking helps you measure your progress and alignment effectively.

Why It Works

Neurofeedback connects you to your mind's patterns, helping you recognize what states of energy and focus support your manifestation goals. Tracking these insights over time provides clarity and empowers you to align with the energy needed to achieve your desires.

RED LIGHT JOURNALING

Harness the power of light to elevate your energy and enhance your manifestation practice. The **Red Light Journaling** integrates **Red Light Therapy**, a technique known for its physical and emotional healing properties, with intentional reflection to align your energy and focus.

How It Works

Red Light Therapy uses gentle, low-wavelength light to stimulate cellular energy, reduce stress, and improve overall well-being. Combining this practice with mindful reflection allows you to connect more deeply with your intentions while enhancing mental clarity and physical vitality.

Steps to Practice Red Light Journaling:

1. **Set Up Your Space:** Choose a quiet, relaxing environment with access to a Red Light Therapy device. Ensure you're comfortable and uninterrupted.
2. **Set Your Intention:** Begin with a clear focus. For example: "I invite healing, clarity, and alignment into my mind and body."
3. **Engage in Red Light Therapy:** Sit or stand comfortably near the light for 10-15 minutes. Breathe deeply and focus on the soothing warmth of the light.
4. **Reflect and Record:** After your session, use your Red Light Journaling to answer prompts like:
   - How did my body feel during the practice?
   - What emotions or thoughts surfaced during this time?
   - How can I align my actions with this sense of renewal and clarity?
5. **Log Your Progress:** Track your sessions, noting any physical or emotional shifts, and observe patterns over time.

Tips for Success:

- Use Red Light Therapy in the morning to energize your day or in the evening for relaxation and healing.
- Pair this activity with affirmations or meditation for deeper alignment.
- Keep reflections simple and focused on how you feel before, during, and after each session.

Why It Works

Red Light Therapy enhances cellular function, improves mood, and reduces stress—creating the ideal conditions for manifestation. By combining this with focused reflection, you amplify your energy, clarity, and alignment with your intentions.

EARTH JOURNALING

Grounding yourself in nature is a simple yet powerful way to reconnect with the energy around you and align with your intentions. The **Earth Journaling** allows you to clear emotional clutter, release stress, and restore balance by tapping into the stabilizing energy of the Earth.

How It Works:

Grounding, or "earthing," involves connecting physically with nature to realign your energy and bring yourself into the present moment. This practice helps you feel centered, calm, and more attuned to your manifestation goals.

Steps to Practice Earth Connection:

1. **Find a Natural Setting:** Choose a peaceful outdoor environment—like a park, garden, beach, or forest—where you can connect with the Earth.
2. **Remove Your Shoes:** Stand, walk, or sit with your bare feet on the ground to establish a physical connection.
3. **Breathe Deeply:** Inhale slowly and deeply, focusing on the sensations of the Earth beneath you. Imagine its energy flowing upward, grounding and stabilizing your body.
4. **Set Your Intention:** While connecting to the Earth, silently affirm: "I release what no longer serves me and welcome balance, clarity, and abundance into my life."
5. **Reflect and Write:** After your practice, reflect on your experience using prompts like:
    - What emotions or sensations did I notice while grounding?
    - How does reconnecting with nature shift my mindset or energy?
    - What steps can I take to stay grounded in my manifestation journey?
6. **Repeat Regularly:** Practice grounding consistently to clear energy blocks and enhance your connection to your intentions.

Tips for Success:

- Try this practice in different natural settings to see where you feel most connected.
- Pair grounding with visualization or affirmations for amplified results.
- If outdoor access is limited, use houseplants, natural stones, or grounding mats to simulate the experience.

Why It Works:

The Earth's energy has a calming and stabilizing effect, helping you release stress and regain focus. By grounding yourself, you create space for clarity and alignment, essential for manifesting your desires.

ENERGY CULTIVATION PRACTICES

Movement is a powerful way to release stagnant energy and align your mind, body, and spirit. The **Energy Cultivation Practices** draws inspiration from **Tai Chi**, a practice that uses gentle, intentional movements to create balance, improve energy flow, and enhance focus—key elements for successful manifestation.

Learn with the ManiFAST™ App

For a guided experience, access instructional videos in the **ManiFAST™ App**. These easy-to-follow videos demonstrate movements you can easily follow at home to align your energy and elevate your manifestation practice.

Simply scan the QR code below to start your Flow Energy Routine and experience the transformative power of movement.

How It Works:

The slow, mindful movements of Tai Chi cultivate a sense of calm, clarity, and centeredness. By incorporating this practice into your daily routine, you can release energetic blocks, improve your focus, and align your actions with your intentions.

Steps to Practice Energy Cultivation Practices:

1. **Set Your Space:** Find a quiet, open area where you can move freely without distractions.
2. **Ground Yourself**: Begin with a few deep breaths to center your energy and set your intention. For example: "I allow energy to flow freely through my mind, body, and spirit."
3. **Practice Gentle Movements:** Flow through the following Tai Chi-inspired exercises:
    - **Energy Sweep:** Stand tall, sweeping your arms upward as you inhale, and letting them float downward as you exhale. Imagine clearing negative energy.
    - **Open & Close:** With palms facing each other, move your arms out to the sides as you inhale, and bring them together slowly as you exhale. Visualize drawing energy inward.
    - **Flowing Water:** Step side-to-side in a slow, rhythmic motion, moving your arms as if guiding water. Feel the flow of energy through your body.
4. **Stay Present:** Focus on the sensation of movement, your breath, and the calm energy flowing within you.
5. **Reflect and Align:** After completing the routine, sit quietly and reflect:
    - How does my body feel after this practice?
    - What thoughts or insights emerged as I moved?
    - How can I carry this sense of flow into my daily intentions?

Tips for Success:

- Move slowly and deliberately, staying fully present with each motion.
- Pair this routine with calming music or practice it outdoors for an enhanced grounding experience.
- If you're short on time, focus on just one or two movements to realign quickly.

Why It Works:

Intentional movement like Tai Chi promotes relaxation, improves focus, and creates harmony between your physical and energetic states. By embodying a sense of flow, you release resistance and open yourself to the energy needed to manifest your goals effortlessly.

MEDITATIVE JOURNALING

Your mind is a powerful landscape where thoughts, emotions, and intentions take shape. **Meditative Journaling** combines meditation with reflective journaling to deepen self-awareness, release mental clutter, and create a clear space for your manifestations to grow.

How It Works:

By guiding your thoughts through meditation and immediately capturing insights in a journal, you align your conscious and subconscious mind. This practice enhances focus, clarity, and emotional release, creating fertile ground for your intentions.

Steps to Practice Meditative Journaling:

1. **Find a Quiet Space:** Sit comfortably in a peaceful, distraction-free environment. Have your journal and pen nearby, ready for reflection.
2. **Begin with Guided Meditation:** Close your eyes and focus on your breath. Use guided meditation, calming music, or visualize a peaceful setting like a meadow or ocean. Spend 5-10 minutes quieting your thoughts and observing your inner world.
3. **Explore Your Mindscape:** Allow images, thoughts, and emotions to surface naturally. Ask yourself:
    - What do I see, feel, or hear in this mental space?
    - Are there any recurring symbols, patterns, or insights?
4. **Start Journaling:** Open your eyes and record your experience, using prompts like:
    - What thoughts or feelings emerged during the meditation?
    - What insights did I gain about my intentions and focus?
    - How can I use this clarity to take the next step toward my goals?
5. **Close with Gratitude:** End your session by writing one or two things you're grateful for. This seals your practice with positive energy.

Tips for Success:

- If your mind wanders during meditation, gently bring your focus back to your breath or chosen visualization.
- Journaling doesn't need to be perfect—write freely without judgment.
- Practice consistently to notice deeper insights and recurring themes over time.

Why It Works:

Meditative Journaling clears mental fog and allows your subconscious mind to communicate powerful messages. By combining meditation with reflection, you gain clarity, align with your intentions, and create a deeper connection to your manifestation goals.

SELF MANIFESTATION

Manifestation requires clarity, direction, and action. **Self Manifestation** is a structured framework that helps you set clear, actionable steps toward achieving your goals. By breaking down your intentions into manageable actions, you create a roadmap that empowers you to move forward with confidence and purpose.

How It Works:

This practice involves defining your goals, identifying the resources you need, and outlining the steps to bring your intentions into reality. Mapping your empowerment journey provides clarity, builds momentum, and keeps you accountable.

Steps to Create Your Self Manifestation:

1. **Define Your Vision:** Write down your primary intention or goal. Be specific and clear.
    - Example: "I manifest a fulfilling new career that aligns with my passion for helping others."
2. **Identify Your Why:** Reflect on why this goal is important to you. Ask yourself:
    - What will achieving this goal bring into my life?
    - How will it positively impact others or my future?
3. **Break It into Steps:** Outline small, actionable steps needed to achieve your goal. Start with the first step and work your way forward. For example:
    - Step 1: Update my resume to reflect my new skills.
    - Step 2: Research job opportunities aligned with my purpose.
    - Step 3: Network with individuals in my desired field.
4. **Identify Resources and Support:** Write down what tools, skills, or support you need to succeed.
    - Example: "I need to take a short online course to build my expertise."
5. **Set Deadlines:** Assign realistic deadlines for each step to maintain accountability and focus.
    - Example: "I will update my resume by the end of this week."
6. **Reflect and Adjust:** Regularly review your map, celebrate progress, and adjust steps as needed. Use prompts like:
    - What progress have I made so far?
    - What challenges have I overcome, and how can I improve?

Tips for Success:

- Start with one goal at a time to avoid being overwhelmed.
- Use visual elements like diagrams, bullet points, or flowcharts to make your map easy to follow.
- Pair this practice with affirmations to strengthen your focus and self-belief.
- Review your map weekly to stay aligned and motivated.

Why It Works:

Self Manifestation transforms big goals into achievable steps, giving you clarity, direction, and a sense of purpose. By following this structured approach, you not only visualize your intentions but take consistent action to manifest them.

COLLECTIVE MANIFESTATION

Manifestation becomes even more powerful when intentions are shared and amplified by collective energy. **Collective Manifestation** helps you align with others to co-create shared goals, combining individual focus into a unified force that accelerates the manifestation process.

How It Works:

When people come together with aligned intentions, their collective energy magnifies the power of each person's focus. This practice is designed for friends, family, or like-minded groups to set shared goals, foster connection, and support one another in the manifestation journey.

Steps to Practice the Collective Manifestation:

1. **Gather Your Group:** Form a group with individuals who share a similar mindset or purpose. This could be a family circle, a group of friends, or a manifestation-focused community.
2. **Clarify the Shared Goal:** Together, identify a collective intention. Be clear and specific. For example:
   - "We intend to cultivate abundance, positivity, and success for our group's endeavors."
3. **Set Individual Contributions:** Each member defines their role or contribution to achieving the goal. Ask:
   - What action can I take to support this shared intention?
   - How can I align my personal goals with the group's vision?
4. **Create a Unified Intention Statement:** Write a statement that combines everyone's focus into one powerful affirmation. For example:
   - "As a group, we amplify our energy to manifest abundance, clarity, and opportunities for all."
5. **Plan Regular Connection Sessions:** Set times to meet virtually or in person to check progress, share experiences, and realign your energy. Use practices like:
   - Group meditation or visualization sessions.
   - Sharing successes and challenges to encourage and uplift one another.
6. **Document Progress:** Use a planner or journal to track collective efforts, breakthroughs, and synchronicities that arise along the way.

Reflection Prompts:

- What progress have we made as a group toward our intention?
- How has my energy been supported or uplifted by the collective focus?
- What shifts or synchronicities have I noticed since aligning with this group intention?

Tips for Success:

- Foster a supportive and non-judgmental environment within your group.
- Encourage open communication, mutual accountability, and celebration of wins (big or small).
- Pair group sessions with shared affirmations or breathwork to strengthen collective energy.

Why It Works:

When people unite with aligned intentions, their combined energy creates a powerful synergy. By pooling focus, effort, and support, the manifestation process accelerates, creating greater momentum and deeper alignment for everyone involved.

VISUALIZATION METHOD

Clarity is the key to manifesting your desires. The **Visualization Method** helps you create a vivid, multi-sensory visualization of your goals, turning abstract intentions into clear, focused mental images. By engaging all your senses, you align your mind and energy with your desired reality.

How It Works:

Visualization is more than just imagining your goals—it's about fully immersing yourself in the experience as if it's already happening. This practice encourages you to refine your vision in detail, making it feel real, tangible, and achievable.

Steps to Practice Visualization Method:

1. **Set Your Space:** Find a quiet, comfortable place free from distractions. Have a journal, pen, and any inspiring tools like images, music, or vision board materials.
2. **Clarify Your Goal:** Write down the intention or goal you want to visualize. Be specific and include details like:
   - What does achieving this goal look like?
   - How will it make you feel?
   - Who is with you, and what are you doing?
3. **Engage Your Senses:** Close your eyes and immerse yourself in the visualization:
   - **Sight:** What do you see? Colors, people, or places?
   - **Sound:** What can you hear at this moment? Voices, nature, music?
   - **Touch:** What physical sensations do you feel (e.g., warmth, textures)?
   - **Smell:** Are there any scents in this scene (e.g., fresh air, flowers, or food)?
   - **Taste:** Is there anything you can taste (e.g., success, celebration, or comfort)?
4. **Write Down the Details:** After visualizing, journal every detail you experienced. Use prompts like:
   - What was most vivid in my visualization?
   - How did I feel during this experience?
   - What steps can I take now to move closer to this vision?
5. **Refine Your Vision Over Time:** Repeat this exercise regularly to deepen and clarify your visualization, adding new layers of detail each time.

Tips for Success:

- Practice visualization during quiet moments, like mornings or evenings, to maximize focus.
- Combine this exercise with calming music or guided meditation to enhance the experience.
- Pair your vision detailing with a vision board or affirmations to reinforce your focus.

Why It Works:

When you vividly visualize your goals with all your senses, your brain begins to perceive them as real, activating your energy and focus toward achieving them. This process strengthens your belief in the possibility of your desires and aligns you with the actions needed to manifest them.

AFFIRMATIONS EMBEDDING METHOD

Affirmations are more than just words; they're powerful statements that reprogram your mind, align your energy, and reinforce your manifestation goals. When paired with harmonic sounds, such as binaural beats or solfeggio frequencies, affirmations become even more impactful by deepening their resonance and effectiveness.

How It Works

Affirmations shift your thoughts and emotions toward positivity and confidence, while harmonic sounds influence your brainwaves and energy fields. Together, they:

- Rewire your subconscious mind, replacing limiting beliefs with empowering thoughts.
- Elevate your vibrational state, creating an optimal environment for manifestation.
- Enhance focus, relaxation, and emotional alignment with your desires.

Steps to Practice the Affirmations Embedding Method

1. **Identify Limiting Beliefs**
    - Take a moment to reflect on any doubts or negative thoughts holding you back.
    - Write them down.
        - Example: "I'm not capable of achieving my dreams."
2. **Reframe with Empowering Statements**
    - Turn these limiting beliefs into positive affirmations. Use present-tense, emotionally resonant statements such as:
        - "I am capable of achieving everything I set my mind to."
        - "I have all the skills and resources I need to succeed."
        - "I attract abundance and opportunities effortlessly."
3. **Choose a Harmonic Frequency**
    - Select a sound frequency that aligns with your intentions:
        - **396 Hz:** Releases fear and guilt.
        - **528 Hz:** Promotes transformation and miracles.
        - **852 Hz:** Awakens intuition and alignment.
4. **Combine Affirmations with Harmonic Sounds**
    - Find a quiet space and play the chosen sound frequency through headphones for 10-15 minutes.
    - Repeat your affirmations aloud or silently, syncing your words with the rhythm of the sounds.
    - Visualize your desires manifesting as you affirm and listen.
5. **Track Your Shifts**
    - After each session, reflect on your experience after each session using prompts like:
        - How did I feel before, during, and after the session?
        - What insights or emotions surfaced?
        - How has this practice influenced my focus, energy, or mood?

Daily Practice

- **Morning Routine:** Start your day by playing a frequency and affirming your goals to set a positive tone.
- **Evening Routine:** Use this method to wind down, releasing stress and reinforcing your intentions before sleep.
- **Consistency:** Practice daily to build momentum and amplify results.

Why It Works

The combination of affirmations and harmonic sounds aligns your mind, body, and energy with your desires. Affirmations program your thoughts for success, while sound frequencies create a vibrational environment that enhances focus, relaxation, and manifestation. Together, these elements form a powerful tool for transforming your reality.

KEY TAKEAWAYS

Congratulations on completing this hands-on journey through manifestation-enhancing activities! Below is a summary of the essential tools and practices covered in this chapter. Use this as a quick reference to integrate these techniques into your daily routine and amplify your manifestation practice.

1. **Mind Resetting**
   - Cultivate inner stillness and prepare your mind for intentional focus.
2. **Sunrise Journaling**
   - Harness the energy of the sun for clarity, inspiration, and alignment.
3. **Breath Aligning Practice**
   - Use the 4-7-8 breathing technique to calm your mind and balance your energy flow.
4. **Biofeedback**
   - Track your emotional and mental states to measure alignment and identify patterns in your progress.
5. **Red Light Journaling**
   - Integrate Red Light Therapy to rejuvenate your energy and clear mental blocks.
6. **Earth Journaling**
   - Reconnect with nature to restore balance, reduce stress, and ground your energy.
7. **Energy Cultivation Practices**
   - Use Tai Chi-inspired movements to align your body, mind, and energy flow.
8. **Meditative Journaling**
   - Combine meditation with reflective journaling to deepen self-awareness and clarity.
9. **Self Manifestation**
   - Create a structured, step-by-step plan to move toward your goals with confidence.
10. **Collective Manifestation**
    - Collaborate with others to amplify shared goals and create collective energy for manifestation.
11. **Visualization Method**
    - Refine your visualization practice by engaging all your senses for a vivid and powerful vision.
12. **Affirmations Embedding Method**
    - Design personalized affirmations to reprogram limiting beliefs, align your mindset, and amplify their impact with harmonic sound frequencies.

Access in the App

These takeaways are also available in the **ManiFAST™ App**, where you can engage with interactive Q&A prompts, receive personalized suggestions, and track your progress. Scan the QR code to dive deeper into your manifestation journey.

Final Reflection

- Which activities resonated most with me, and why?
- How can I incorporate these tools into my daily routine for greater consistency?
- What shifts have I noticed in my mindset, energy, or progress toward my goals?

By integrating these activities into your manifestation journey, you now possess a toolkit designed to enhance your alignment, focus, and energy. Continue exploring, experimenting, and combining these techniques to discover what works best for you.

The power to manifest your desires is within you—stay intentional, stay aligned, and trust the process!

chapter Nine

HARNESSING THE INTERNAL COMPASS

INTRODUCTION

Your intuition is your internal compass, guiding you toward alignment, clarity, and purpose. When you learn to listen to its subtle signals, you tap into a deep source of wisdom that can simplify your manifestation journey. In this chapter, you'll explore how to tune into your intuition, identify resistance and flow states, and streamline your approach to achieving your goals.

Manifestation doesn't need to be complicated. **When you trust yourself and learn to recognize moments of your alignment—or when resistance is holding you back**—you can navigate your path with greater ease and confidence. This chapter focuses on simplifying your manifestation process, removing unnecessary obstacles, and amplifying the natural flow of energy toward your desires.

Here's what we'll cover:

- **Tuning Into Your Intuition:** Learn how to trust and strengthen your inner guidance system.
- **Identifying Resistance and Flow States:** Recognize when you're in alignment and how to release resistance.
- **Simplifying Your Manifestation Process:** Practical techniques to streamline your approach and focus on what matters most.
- **Quiz: Are You Following Your Compass?:** A quick assessment to measure how well you're using your intuition.
- **Key Takeaways:** A summary of insights to help you harness your internal compass effectively.

By the end of this chapter, you'll have the tools to clarify your goals and build a mindset that supports your manifestation journey. Let's get started with exploring how self-awareness can transform the way you create your reality.

TUNING INTO YOUR INTUITION

Your intuition is the quiet voice within, offering guidance, insight, and clarity. It's not bound by logic or external noise—it's a deep, inner knowing that aligns you with your highest self and goals. **Tuning into your intuition** allows you to make decisions that feel right, recognize opportunities, and manifest with greater ease.

How It Works:

Intuition often speaks through feelings, subtle nudges, and sudden insights. The key to harnessing its power lies in quieting the mind, noticing its signals, and learning to trust it.

Steps to Tune Into Your Intuition:

1. **Create Stillness:**
    - Find a quiet space where you can sit comfortably without distractions.
    - Close your eyes, take slow, deep breaths, and let go of any tension or racing thoughts.
2. **Ask a Question:**
    - Focus on a specific area of your life or manifestation journey where you seek guidance.
    - Silently ask yourself: "What is my next aligned step?" or "What feels right for me right now?"
3. **Notice the Signals:**
    - Pay attention to any sensations, feelings, or images that come up. Intuition often communicates through:
        - A gut feeling (a sense of knowing or unease).
        - Flashes of insight or ideas that seem to come out of nowhere.
        - Physical sensations, like lightness or heaviness in your body.
4. **Journal Your Insights:**
    - Write down anything you noticed, no matter how subtle. Use prompts like:
        - What feelings or thoughts surfaced as I tuned in?
        - What message or direction did I receive?
        - How can I act on this guidance?
5. **Strengthen Trust Through Action:**
    - Take a small step based on your intuitive insight, even if it feels uncertain. Trusting and acting on intuition builds confidence in its accuracy over time.

Tips for Success:

- Practice daily stillness or meditation to strengthen your connection with your intuition.
- Avoid overanalyzing; intuition feels natural, not forced.
- Trust your first impressions—intuition often speaks before the mind interferes.
- Combine intuitive insights with aligned action to amplify your manifestation results.

Why It Works:

Your intuition connects you to your subconscious mind, where your deepest wisdom and desires reside. By tuning in and acting on its guidance, you align your energy with the most effortless and inspired path toward your goals.

Practice with the ManiFAST™ App

Use the **app** to enhance this practice with guided meditations, including the "Finding Your Internal Compass" session. The app offers real-time AI guidance, asking reflective questions like:

- “What do you notice?”
- “How does it feel?”

These sessions are designed to help you tune into your intuition and deepen your connection with your inner compass. Simply scan the QR code to begin your guided meditation and unlock your intuitive potential.

Identifying Resistance and Flow States

Manifestation is not just about action; it's about recognizing when you're in alignment with the natural flow of energy—or when resistance is holding you back. Resistance feels heavy, frustrating, and stagnant, while flow states are light, effortless, and filled with momentum. By learning to identify both, you can release blocks and return to a state where manifestation feels natural and rewarding.

Understanding Resistance

Resistance arises when your thoughts, emotions, or actions are misaligned with your desires. It can manifest as procrastination, self-doubt, or a feeling of being “stuck.”

- **Signs of Resistance:**
  - Feeling drained or unmotivated.
  - Negative self-talk or limiting beliefs.
  - Physical tension, anxiety, or discomfort when focusing on a goal.
  - Avoidance of tasks or actions related to your intentions.

Understanding Flow States

Flow is the opposite of resistance. It's the state where your actions, energy, and intentions are in perfect harmony, and progress feels effortless. In flow, you're fully present, inspired, and productive.

- **Signs of Flow:**
  - A sense of ease, joy, and inspiration while taking action.
  - Feeling energized and fully absorbed in the moment.
  - Tasks feel natural, time moves quickly, and ideas come easily.
  - A deep sense of trust and alignment with your goals.

Steps to Identify and Shift Resistance to Flow

1. **Pause and Reflect:**
   - When you feel stuck, pause to check in with yourself. Ask:
     - What am I feeling right now—physically, mentally, and emotionally?
     - What thoughts or beliefs are creating resistance?
2. **Release the Resistance:**
   - Acknowledge and accept the resistance without judgment. Then, release it using techniques like:
     - Breathwork: Try the 4-7-8 breathing technique to calm your nervous system.
     - Reframing Beliefs: Replace limiting thoughts with empowering affirmations.
     - Movement: Shake off stagnation with light physical activity (e.g., stretching or walking).
3. **Identify Flow Moments:**
   - Think back to times when you felt deeply inspired and aligned. Ask yourself:
     - What was I doing when I felt in flow?
     - What thoughts, environment, or actions contributed to that state?
4. **Recreate Flow Conditions:**
   - Build an environment that encourages flow:
     - Remove distractions and simplify tasks.
     - Set intentions for focus and ease before starting any activity.
     - Incorporate practices like visualization, meditation, or affirmations to align your energy.
5. **Celebrate Small Wins:**
   - Progress builds momentum. Acknowledge even the smallest steps to strengthen your flow state.

Reflection Prompts:

- Where am I currently experiencing resistance in my life?
- What small shift can I make to create ease and flow?
- What does being in flow feel like for me, and how can I get back there?

Why It Works:

By recognizing and addressing resistance, you clear space for alignment and flow. Flow states amplify your focus, energy, and creativity, making manifestation feel natural, joyful, and effortless.

SIMPLIFYING YOUR MANIFESTATION PROCESS

Manifestation doesn't have to be complicated. While it's natural to overthink, over-plan, or feel overwhelmed by endless techniques, simplicity often creates the greatest results. By streamlining your approach, focusing on what works, and removing distractions, you can make manifestation more effective, enjoyable, and aligned.

Steps to Simplify Your Manifestation Process

1. **Clarify Your Core Desires:**
    - Simplification begins with focus. Write down your top 1-3 intentions—goals that matter most to you right now.
    - Ask yourself:
        - What do I truly desire at this moment?
        - Why is this important to me?
    - Eliminate goals that feel forced, unrealistic, or out of alignment with your current energy.
2. **Prioritize Techniques That Work for You:**
    - Not every manifestation tool resonates with everyone. Reflect on the techniques that bring you clarity and results:
        - Visualization?
        - Affirmations?
        - Meditation or journaling?
    - Choose 2-3 core practices and commit to them consistently. Trust that simplicity leads to deeper alignment.
3. **Take Inspired, Focused Action:**
    - Break your manifestation process into small, manageable steps. Ask yourself:
        - What is one action I can take today to move closer to my intention?
    - Avoid overwhelm by focusing only on the next step, not the entire journey.
4. **Create Space for Alignment:**
    - Overthinking can block flow. Simplify your mind and energy with these practices:
        - **Daily Stillness:** Spend 5-10 minutes in quiet reflection or meditation.
        - **Let Go of Outcomes:** Release attachment to how your desires will manifest.
        - **Declutter Your Space:** Clear physical spaces to invite clarity and flow into your life.
5. **Trust and Repeat:**
    - Simplifying doesn't mean you're doing less—it means you're doing what works with trust and intention.
    - Repeat simple affirmations like:
        - "I trust the process. Everything I need is unfolding effortlessly."
    - "My energy flows easily toward what I desire."

Reflection Prompts:

- Which manifestation techniques bring me the most clarity and alignment?
- What unnecessary steps or distractions can I let go of?
- How can I simplify my approach while staying intentional and consistent?

Why It Works:

Simplicity clears mental and emotional clutter, allowing you to focus your energy on what truly matters. When you align with clear, intentional action, manifestation becomes a natural and effortless process.

QUIZ

ARE YOU FOLLOWING YOUR COMPASS?

This short quiz helps you assess how well you're tuning into your intuition, identifying flow states, and simplifying your manifestation process. By reflecting on your current habits and mindset, you'll gain clarity on where you're aligned and where there might be room for improvement.

You can complete this quiz right here in the workbook or take it in the **ManiFAST™ App**, where you'll receive additional insights and guidance based on your responses. Simply scan the QR code to access the interactive quiz and track your progress.

Reflection Questions

- Which areas of my manifestation process feel most aligned right now?
- Where do I notice resistance, and how can I shift back into flow?
- What small changes can I make to follow my internal compass more consistently?

Reflection

KEY TAKEAWAYS

In this chapter, you've learned to harness the power of your internal compass—your intuition—to simplify your manifestation process and align more deeply with your desires. Here's a quick recap of the key insights:

1. **Tuning Into Your Intuition**
    - Your intuition is your internal guide, offering clarity and direction.
    - Create moments of stillness, trust your first impressions, and take inspired action based on your intuitive insights.
2. **Identifying Resistance and Flow States**
    - Resistance feels heavy and blocks your progress, while flow states bring ease, clarity, and inspiration.
    - Recognize resistance, release it with tools like breathwork and reframing, and create conditions that encourage flow.
3. **Simplifying Your Manifestation Process**
    - Focus on what matters most by clarifying your top 1-3 goals.
    - Streamline your techniques, take small inspired actions, and trust the process to unfold naturally.
4. **Quiz: Are You Following Your Compass?**
    - Assess how well you're aligning with your intuition, flow states, and simplified practices.
    - Reflect on where you can fine-tune your habits to strengthen your alignment.

Access in the App

These takeaways are also available in the **ManiFAST™ App**, where you can engage with interactive Q&A prompts, review personalized suggestions, and track your progress. Scan the QR code to dive deeper into your manifestation journey.

Final Reflection:

- How can I trust my intuition more deeply in my manifestation journey?
- What steps will I take to simplify my approach and reduce resistance?
- How does it feel when I'm fully in flow and aligned with my goals?

By learning to trust your internal compass, you've unlocked the ability to navigate your manifestation journey with ease, clarity, and confidence. When you simplify, listen

chapter

Ten

YOUR MANIFESTATION JOURNEY BEGINS

INTRODUCTION

Congratulations! You've reached the final chapter of this workbook, but in truth, this is where your manifestation journey truly begins. The tools, strategies, and insights you've explored along the way have already laid the foundation for the life you've been dreaming of. You've cultivated clarity, confidence, and alignment, and now it's time to put all that into practice as you move forward with intention.

This chapter is an opportunity to reflect on your growth, commit to your future self, and solidify your readiness to manifest with intention and trust. You've already taken powerful steps toward aligning your energy, refining your goals, and overcoming challenges. Now, it's time to step forward with confidence, fully embodying the version of yourself that turns dreams into reality.

Here's what we'll cover:

- **Reflecting on Your Growth:** A look back at the progress, insights, and transformation you've achieved.
- **Goal Setting:** Commit to Your Future Self: A final exercise to define and commit to the intentions you're ready to manifest.
- **Final Words of Encouragement:** Inspiration to empower and uplift you as you move forward.
- **Quiz: Your Manifestation Readiness:** A self-assessment to ensure you're stepping into your journey with clarity and confidence.
- **Key Takeaways:** A final summary to anchor the most important insights and prepare you for what comes next.

As you prepare to step into the next chapter of your life, remember this: manifestation is not a single destination—it's a journey of growth, alignment, and becoming. Trust yourself, trust the process, and embrace the endless possibilities that await.

You're ready for this next step, so let's begin!

REFLECTING ON YOUR GROWTH

Reflection is a powerful tool for recognizing how far you've come, celebrating your progress, and acknowledging the transformation you've experienced. By looking back at the shifts in your mindset, energy, and actions, you strengthen your belief in yourself and your ability to manifest your desires.

This practice allows you to honor your journey, see the challenges you've overcome, and embrace the growth that has brought you to this moment.

Steps to Reflect on Your Growth

1. **Celebrate Your Wins**
    - Take a moment to list the accomplishments, big or small, that you've achieved during this process.
    - Reflection Prompts:
        - What intentions or goals have I already begun to manifest?
        - What positive changes have I noticed in my thoughts, energy, or habits?
        - What am I most proud of in my journey so far?
2. **Recognize the Challenges You Overcame**
    - Acknowledge the obstacles, doubts, and fears you've worked through. This helps you see your resilience and how much you've grown as a result.
    - Reflection Prompts:
        - What challenges or blocks did I face, and how did I overcome them?
        - What have these experiences taught me about myself?
        - How did overcoming these challenges make me stronger or clearer in my vision?
3. **Identify Your Shifts**
    - Reflect on the shifts in your mindset, energy, and confidence throughout this journey. Notice how these shifts have impacted your approach to manifestation.
    - Reflection Prompts:
        - What limiting beliefs have I released?
        - How has my mindset or energy improved since I started this process?
        - What new habits or practices have I integrated into my daily life?
4. **Celebrate the Person You're Becoming**
    - Take a moment to honor the version of yourself who is committed to growth, alignment, and trust. You've already come so far.
    - Affirm: "I honor the progress I've made and embrace the person I am becoming."
5. **Journal Your Growth**
    - Summarize your reflections in your journal or workbook. Use these prompts to guide your writing:
        - What have I learned about myself during this manifestation journey?
        - What moments or breakthroughs stand out as the most transformative?
        - How will I use this growth as I continue manifesting my goals?

Why It Works

Reflecting on your growth shifts your focus from what's missing to how much you've achieved. It builds confidence, gratitude, and momentum, reminding you that manifestation is not just about achieving goals, but about the journey of becoming who you're meant to be—one that you're already succeeding at.

GOAL SETTING

COMMIT TO YOUR FUTURE SELF

Your future self is the version of you who has already achieved your goals, aligned with your desires, and embraced your highest potential. By connecting with and committing to this future version of yourself, you anchor your intentions and take deliberate action toward becoming who you're meant to be.

Steps to Set Goals and Commit to Your Future Self

1. **Visualize Your Future Self**
   - Close your eyes and take a few deep breaths. Imagine the version of yourself who has already achieved your manifestation goals.
   - Reflect on the details:
     - What does this version of you look like?
     - How do you feel, think, and act?
     - What does your life look like, and what has changed?
2. **Write a Letter to Your Future Self**
   - Write a heartfelt letter to your future self as if you're already living the life you desire. Express gratitude, confidence, and excitement.
   - Prompts to include:
     - What intentions or goals did you commit to that brought you here?
     - How did you overcome challenges and stay aligned with your vision?
     - How do you feel now that you've achieved this version of yourself?
3. **Set Specific and Aligned Goals**
   - Break your vision into clear, actionable goals. Focus on 1-3 major intentions that feel aligned and achievable.
   - Use the SMART goal framework:
     - **S**pecific: Define your goals clearly.
     - **M**easurable: Identify how you'll track progress.
     - **A**chievable: Ensure they are realistic and inspiring.
     - **R**elevant: Align them with your vision and values.
     - **T**ime-bound: Set a timeline for achieving them.
4. **Example:**
   - "I commit to launching my creative project within 6 months, focusing on consistent weekly progress to bring my vision to life."

5. **Create a Commitment Statement**
    - Write a personal statement affirming your commitment to your future self and your goals. For example:
    - "I commit to taking inspired, aligned actions every day to become the person I know I am capable of being. My future self is already waiting for me, and I trust the process to get there."
6. **Take the First Step**
    - Identify the next small step you can take toward your goal today. Break the journey into manageable actions to build momentum and confidence.

Reflection Prompts

- Who is the version of me I am committing to becoming?
- What goals am I ready to focus on and commit to fully?
- What actions will I take to honor this commitment to myself?

Why It Works

By committing to your future self, you're not just setting goals; you're strengthening your belief in your ability to achieve your goals. Aligning your vision with clear intentions and actionable steps transforms dreams into reality and creates a path for you to walk with confidence.

FINAL WORDS OF ENCOURAGEMENT

As you come to the end of this workbook, remember that your manifestation journey is just beginning. The tools, insights, and practices you've explored are now part of your foundation—ready to support you as you step into the life you've envisioned.

Manifestation is not about perfection; it's about progress. It's about showing up for yourself, trusting the process, and staying open to the possibilities that await you. Challenges will arise, and that's okay—every setback is a lesson, every obstacle an opportunity to grow stronger, clearer, and more aligned.

You are capable and the life you're dreaming of is already on its way.

A Few Reminders for Your Journey

1. **Trust Yourself**
    - You already have everything you need within you. Trust your intuition, your energy, and your ability to bring your desires to life.
2. **Celebrate Your Progress**
    - Manifestation is a journey, not a race. Every small step, every shift in mindset, and every moment of growth matters. Celebrate how far you've come and trust where you're going.
3. **Stay Open and Flexible**
    - The universe often delivers your desires in ways you can't predict. Stay open to surprises, synchronicities, and opportunities that align with your vision.
4. **You Are Always Manifesting**
    - Every thought, feeling, and action contributes to your reality. When you align your energy with your desires and take inspired action, you create a life of purpose, joy, and abundance.
5. **You Are Capable and Worthy**
    - There are no limits to what you can achieve. No dream is too big, and no goal is out of reach. You are worthy of your desires, and you are capable of creating the life you want.

Affirmation for the Journey Ahead

"I trust the process, believe in my abilities, and welcome my manifestations into my life with gratitude and joy. Everything I desire is already on its way to me."

Final Reflection:

- What have I learned about myself during this journey?
- What is the one goal I'm most excited to pursue now?
- How will I celebrate myself and stay aligned with my vision moving forward?

Take a moment to honor the growth, clarity, and confidence you've cultivated. Your journey doesn't end here—it begins now, as you step forward with trust, intention, and belief in yourself.

QUIZ

YOUR MANIFESTATION READINESS

This final quiz helps you reflect on how prepared and aligned you are to step into the next phase of your manifestation journey. It allows you to assess your mindset, energy, and actions, ensuring you are fully ready to manifest your desires with clarity and confidence.

Take this quiz exclusively in the **ManiFAST™ App** to gain detailed insights and personalized guidance based on your responses. Scan the QR code below to access the interactive quiz and track your progress.

Reflection Questions

- What areas of this quiz show my greatest strengths?
- Where do I need to focus more to prepare myself for success?
- What is one small step I can take today to strengthen my readiness?

Reflection

"

I am ready to MANIFEST my desires with trust, clarity, and confidence. I align my energy, take INSPIRED action, and trust the process to unfold perfectly.

AFFIRMATION FOR READINESS

KEY TAKEAWAYS

This final chapter marks the beginning of a lifelong journey of growth, alignment, and creation. By reflecting on your progress, committing to your future self, and embracing trust, you are now equipped to manifest with clarity, confidence, and purpose.

1. **Reflecting on Your Growth**
   - Celebrate the progress you've made and acknowledge the transformations you've experienced.
   - Acknowledge the challenges you've overcome and the transformation you've experienced.
2. **Goal Setting: Commit to Your Future Self**
   - Visualize your future self and align your goals with who you want to become.
   - Set clear, actionable intentions and commit to taking steps toward your vision.
3. **Final Words of Encouragement**
   - Trust yourself, trust the process, and celebrate every step of the journey.
   - Remember that setbacks are opportunities for growth, and you are capable of achieving anything you desire.
4. **Quiz: Your Manifestation Readiness**
   - Assess your mindset, energy, and actions to ensure you're ready to step into the next phase of your journey.
   - Reflect on areas where you are thriving and where you can realign for deeper success.

Access in the App

These takeaways are also available in the **ManiFAST™ App**, where you can engage with interactive Q&A prompts, review personalized suggestions, and track your progress. Scan the QR code to dive deeper into your manifestation journey.

Final Reflection:

- How will I honor my growth and progress moving forward?
- What daily actions will I take to stay aligned with my vision?
- How will I celebrate the life I am manifesting as it unfolds?

With this, your journey toward manifestation continues. The tools, reflections, and practices in this workbook are yours to revisit and refine as you grow. Remember that manifestation is not just about achieving goals—it's about becoming the person who lives the life they've envisioned. The tools and reflections in this workbook are yours to revisit and refine as you grow.

The universe is working with you, and the possibilities are limitless.

Conclusion

CONCLUSION

Congratulations on completing this manifestation workbook! With it, you have taken intentional steps to explore your desires, overcome challenges, and align your energy, actions, and mindset with the life you're ready to create.

Manifestation is not just about reaching a destination—it's about the journey of becoming the best version of yourself. Through reflection, daily practices, and a deeper connection to your intentions, you've built a strong foundation for manifesting the life you envision.

What You've Accomplished

- **Clarity:** You've gained a clear understanding of your goals, intentions, and desires.
- **Tools and Strategies:** You've explored techniques to shift your mindset, raise your energy, and build consistent routines that support your manifestation practice.
- **Growth:** You've reflected on limiting beliefs, overcome blocks, and aligned with the flow of abundance and possibility.

Each chapter has given you the knowledge and tools you need to transform dreams into reality. Now, the next steps are in your hands.

Moving Forward

1. **Trust the Process**
   - Stay open to the unexpected. Manifestation often unfolds in ways we cannot predict. Trust that every step brings you closer to your desires.
2. **Stay Consistent**
   - Commit to the practices, routines, and tools that resonate with you. Small, consistent actions build momentum over time.
3. **Celebrate Your Progress**
   - Honor every step you take, every breakthrough you experience, and every win—big or small. Celebrate how far you've come and where you're going.
4. **Embrace Flexibility and Growth**
   - As your goals evolve, stay open to realigning them. Flexibility is a sign of growth—trust that your desires are constantly shifting to match your highest potential.

Final Words of Encouragement

You are powerful, capable, and worthy of manifesting the life you desire. Everything you need is already within you—trust your intuition, take inspired action, and remain open to the limitless possibilities that the universe has to offer.

Remember:

- You are always manifesting.
- The universe responds to your energy, beliefs, and actions.
- Your journey is unique—trust yourself every step of the way.

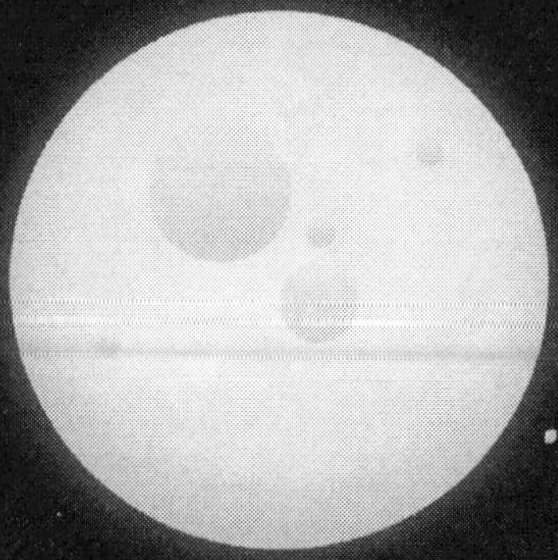

FINAL AFFIRMATION

"I am open, aligned, and ready to receive. My desires are manifesting with ease, joy, and abundance."

Thank you for embarking on this transformative journey. Go forward with trust, belief, and the confidence that the life you desire is already on its way to you.

Your manifestation journey begins now.

REFERENCES

1. **Chopra, Deepak.** The Seven Spiritual Laws of Success: A Practical Guide to the Fulfillment of Your Dreams. Amber-Allen Publishing, 1994.
    - Discusses spiritual principles that align with manifestation and intentional living.
2. **Dispenza, Joe.** Breaking the Habit of Being Yourself: How to Lose Your Mind and Create a New One. Hay House, 2012.
    - Explores the science of reprogramming the subconscious mind to create a new reality.
3. **Gawain, Shakti.** Creative Visualization: Use the Power of Your Imagination to Create What You Want in Life. New World Library, 1978.
    - Transformative guide to using visualization techniques to manifest desires.
4. **Greene, Brian.** The Elegant Universe: Superstrings, Hidden Dimensions, and the Quest for the Ultimate Theory. W. W. Norton & Company, 1999.
    - Provides a scientific perspective on string theory and the vibrational nature of the universe.
5. **Goldman, Jonathan.** Healing Sounds: The Power of Harmonics. Healing Arts Press, 2002.
    - Exploration of the transformative power of sound frequencies for healing and manifestation.
6. **Hall, Judy.** The Crystal Bible. Godsfield Press, 2003.
    - Comprehensive guide to using crystals for healing, energy alignment, and manifestation.
7. **Hay, Louise.** You Can Heal Your Life. Hay House, 1984.
    - Life-changing guide on affirmations and the power of positive thinking to transform one's life.
8. **Hill, Napoleon.** Think and Grow Rich. The Ralston Society, 1937.
    - Timeless book on the power of thoughts and goal-setting in achieving success.
9. **Jung, Carl G.** The Archetypes and the Collective Unconscious. Princeton University Press, 1959.
    - Foundational insights into subconscious patterns and their influence on human behavior.
10. **Kam Chuen, Lam.** The Way of Energy: Mastering the Chinese Art of Internal Strength with Chi Kung Exercise. Simon & Schuster, 1991.
    - Practical guide to cultivating energy and balance through Tai Chi exercises.
11. **Louv, Richard.** Last Child in the Woods: Saving Our Children from Nature-Deficit Disorder. Algonquin Books, 2005.
    - Highlights the healing power of nature, relevant to grounding exercises.
12. **Tolle, Eckhart.** The Power of Now: A Guide to Spiritual Enlightenment. New World Library, 1997.
    - Offers insights into mindfulness and present-moment awareness as tools for personal transformation.
13. **Weil, Andrew.** Breathing: The Master Key to Self-Healing. Sounds True, 2004.
    - Powering guide to using breathwork techniques for relaxation and mental clarity.